REBELS, REDS, ...

Rebels, Reds, Radicals is the inaugural volume in PROVOCATIONS, a series of concise works advancing broad arguments, written by authors deeply immersed in their fields.

Rebels, Reds, Radicals also serves as the introduction to *Realms of Freedom*, Ian McKay's forthcoming multi-volume history of socialism and radicalism in Canada.

REBELS, REDS, RADICALS

Rethinking Canada's Left History

Ian McKay

Between the Lines
Toronto, Canada

Rebels, Reds, Radicals

First published in Canada in 2005 by
Between the Lines
720 Bathurst Street, Suite #404
Toronto, Ontario M5S 2R4
1-800-718-7201
www.btlbooks.com

Library and Archives Canada Cataloguing in Publication

McKay, Ian, 1953–
Rebels, reds, radicals : rethinking Canada's left history / Ian McKay.

Includes bibliographical references and index.
ISBN 978-1-896357-97-3

1. Socialism—Canada—History. 2. Canada—Politics and government. 3. Right and left (Political science) I. Title.

HX109.M35 2005 335'.00971 C2005-901528-4

Cover and text design by Jennifer Tiberio
Printed in Canada
Second printing July 2007

Between the Lines gratefully acknowledges assistance for its publishing activities from the Canada Council for the Arts, the Ontario Arts Council, the Government of Ontario through the Ontario Book Publishers Tax Credit program and through the Ontario Book Initiative, and the Government of Canada through the Book Publishing Industry Development Program.

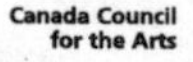

Conseil des Arts
du Canada

Canada

ONTARIO ARTS COUNCIL
CONSEIL DES ARTS DE L'ONTARIO

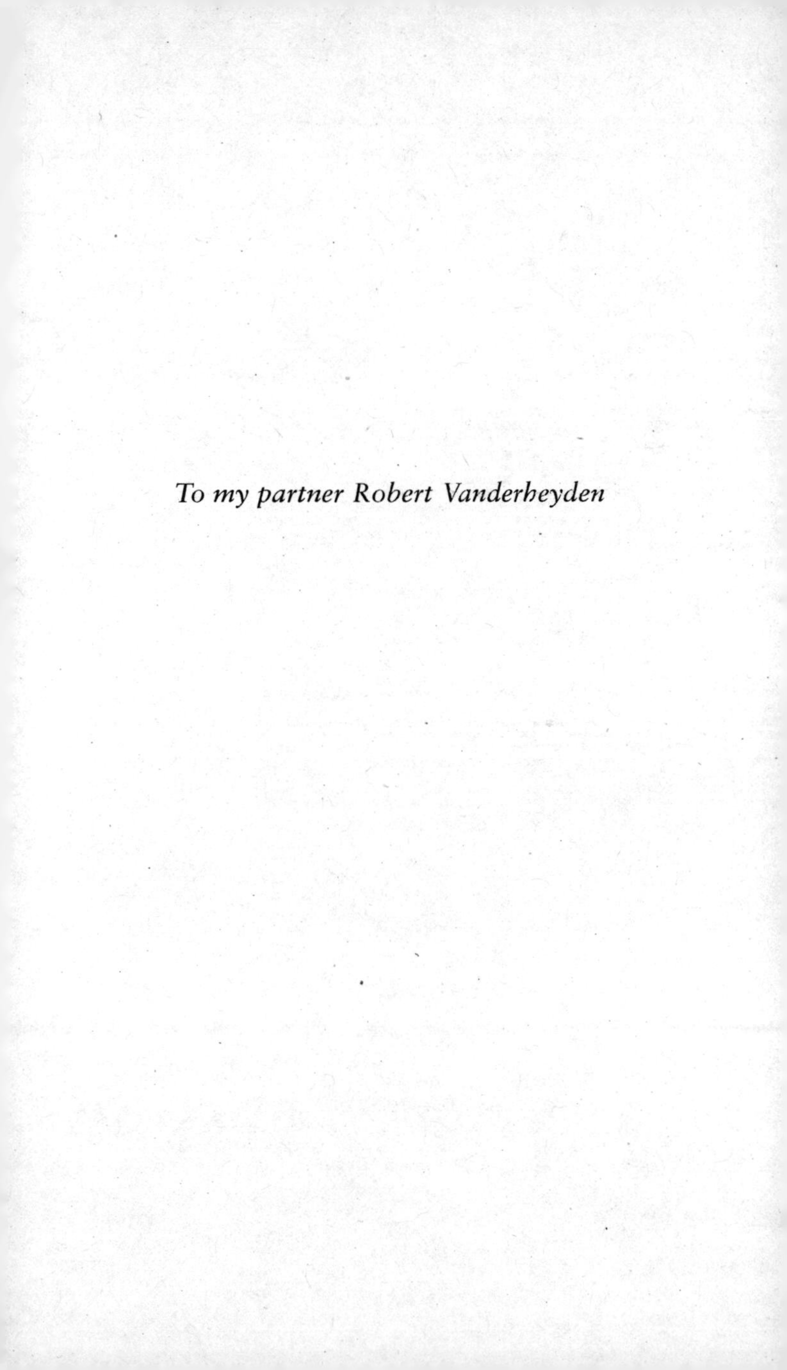

To my partner Robert Vanderheyden

Contents

Acknowledgements

PARTS OF THIS BOOK draw on previously published articles: "The Liberal Order Framework: A Prospectus for a Reconnaissance of Canadian History," *Canadian Historical Review* 81, 3 (September 2000): 617–45; and "For a New Kind of History: A Reconnaissance of 100 Years of Canadian Socialism," *Labour/Le Travail* 46 (Fall 2000): 69–125. I thank the editors of these journals for their permission to use this material.

I would like to thank Carmen Neilson-Varty, Kate Muller, David and Robin McKay, and Amanda Crocker for research assistance. From Between the Lines, Paul Eprile and Jamie Swift have been generous with their encouragement, and Robert Clarke has been a wonderful editor. My good friend Sue Galvin and my sister Kitty Lewis have been great sources of strength. At Queen's University, I owe a special debt to the students in my "History of Canadian Socialism" seminar; they fill me with a sense of the big things that a new generation of leftists in Canada will accomplish.

ONE

Realms of Freedom, Realms of Necessity

IN 1998 THE PLANET'S two hundred wealthiest residents had a net worth equal to about 41 per cent of the total world population. A very few favoured individuals—Bill Gates, the principal owners of Wal-Mart, and the Sultan of Brunei—together enjoyed accumulations of wealth equal to the national incomes of thirty-six of the world's most impoverished countries.

Meanwhile about 1.3 billion people around the world were making do on the equivalent of about one U.S. dollar a day. In Canada, one of the wealthiest countries in the world, poverty increased dramatically from 1990 to 1995, particularly in metropolitan centres. In large cities the general population grew by 6.9 per cent between 1900 and 1995; those with living standards below the Statistics Canada poverty line increased in numbers by 24.5 per cent. Women in Canada are still the poorest of the poor: their pre-tax incomes amount to 62 per cent of men's incomes; they make up a disproportionate share of the population with low incomes—2.4 million in 2001 compared to 1.9 million men. At the turn of the twenty-first century, more than a decade after the House of Commons unanimously passed a dramatic resolution to "seek to eliminate child poverty by the year 2000," about one in every six Canadian children was—according to the state's own statistics—impoverished. At least four out of every ten renter households were paying more than 30 per cent of their monthly incomes on shelter, leaving them little left over for food, transportation, or other basic necessities.[1]

In the first decade of the new century, global warming proceeds at a faster pace than at any time during the past four hundred to six hundred years. Since the beginning of the twentieth century the mean surface temperature of the Earth has increased by about 0.6 degrees Celsius; about half of that warming has taken place in the past forty years. The impact on the Arctic has been striking. Scholars report a 40 per cent reduction in the thickness of the ice pack and new ailments such as lungworms in muskoxen. The global sea level rose faster in the last century than it did in the previous three thousand years. With continued global warming, billions of people face unimaginable calamities. The glacier-fed rivers of the Himalayas, which supply water to one-third of the world's population, are likely to flood. Latin Americans confront the prospect of a severe water shortage.[2]

The forty-two million people who have contracted HIV/AIDS confront, as did the twenty-two million already killed by the disease, crumbling health-care systems and a profit-oriented pharmaceutical industry. In 2003, one country—the United States—voted against a United Nations resolution calling for open access to drugs to meet this "global health emergency."[3]

Globally a vast engine of accumulation transforms almost every human activity into a dollars-and-cents proposition. Across North America cities are penned in by look-alike malls, full of commodities designed to slake recently invented consumer desires. In multiplex movie theatres and supersized grocery stores, consumers are enveloped by a system of goods and services that doubles as a system of meaning and transcendence. Yet all too often there is seemingly no clear purpose or direction to everyday life: activities seem geared to *means* and not to *ends*, to *fragmented* rather than *integrated* experiences, to an eternal "present" and not to any history or future. Struggling for *something* beyond the shopping mall, North Americans grasp at the occult, countless schemes of self-improvement, new diets, "nature"—all of which require further trips to the shopping mall.[4]

This general state of affairs, we are told again and again, every day, by a hundred voices and in a hundred ways, is the only way things can possibly be: all of these massive patterns are beyond human control; you might try to change one or two details, you cannot change the big picture; to imagine a radically different world that does not generate patterns like the ones we are now seeing is to succumb to a delusion.

This "delusion"—that another world is possible—is traditionally called the left.

THE REAL UTOPIA

To be a leftist—a.k.a. socialist, anarchist, radical, global justice activist, communist, socialist-feminist, Marxist, Green, revolutionary—means believing, at a gut level, "It doesn't have to be this way." *Vivre autrement*—"live otherwise! Live in another way!"—was a slogan used by one Quebec radical group in the 1970s. *Reasoning Otherwise* was the slogan of William Irvine, the legendary Prairie socialist. Words like these are inscribed on the heart of every leftist.

Of course, every one of the social problems of the day—from growing inequality to global warming—has its own story. It is properly addressed by its own experts. Such problems cannot simply be lumped together. Each demands its own response. So why not just do what is pragmatically possible, and tackle one issue at a time?

Just so. Living otherwise means engaging with the life-and-death, down-to-earth issues as they present themselves. Living and reasoning otherwise mean the mobilization of resources to handle the emergencies of everyday life.

Yet many people engaged in these emergencies are forced to the conclusion that living otherwise demands more than pragmatic, one-issue-at-a-time responses. Consider the HIV/AIDS pandemic. Suppose, instead of some grandiose scheme of ridding the planet of the disease, you just settle for a more modest objective: reducing the projected death toll over the next few decades, say, from forty-two million to ten million. You come up with the most practical, common-sense ways of doing so: making drugs as effective as possible, promoting the use of safe sex, attacking the other ailments that facilitate the spread of AIDS, and fighting the stigma often attached to people living with the disease. Quite soon you will find yourself up against people who are actively working against you. The Catholic

Church will fight you on "moral" grounds about the human rights of gays and the legitimacy of contraception. Pharmaceutical companies will fight you economically on producing free and effective medicines. The U.S. government, the mightiest in the world, will fight you on both fronts. How are you going to make an effective difference, if your struggle necessarily means working in a world dominated by these forces?

Or suppose, instead of some revolutionary vision of humanity living in a harmonious balance with the rest of nature, you settle for a more modest objective—say, a 50 per cent reduction in carbon-based air pollution over the next ten years. You come up with the most practical, common-sense proposals for doing so: reducing emissions of carbon dioxide, switching 35 per cent of the power grid to alternative energy sources, cutting back on coal-burning generating plants, exploring new energy sources such as wind or solar power. Even though you can argue that every human has a long-term interest in the success of these modest proposals, you will quite quickly find yourself up against people who are actively working against you. Automobile manufacturers will fight your demand that they make only less-polluting cars. Powerful oil companies will hire advertising firms and scientific consultants to discredit you. And, once again, the U.S. government will oppose even the most pragmatic, down-to-earth measures—even if many of its own scientific experts are convinced that a capitalist system reliant on fossil fuels is one that is riding for a fall.

Do what is possible, one issue at a time? Of course—there's no realistic alternative. But you will most likely soon reach conclusions about the patterns of opposition and support that shape each and every one of these issues and connect them together. You may well decide that the persistent general relations *behind* that specific pattern also need to be understood and changed. You will start to see not just a random pattern of problems, but a system underlying them.

Every leftist, at some level, believes and acts on this insight: there are ways of explaining not just the individual problems but the connections between them. Once grasped in thought, these connections have to be transformed in reality. To tackle even one problem—eliminating HIV/AIDS, preventing global environmental meltdown—means struggling to puzzle out why that problem arose in the first place. As soon as you start pursuing the process of figuring each problem out, and connecting it with other problems, you have started down the road to leftism. You will be led, step by step, to a recovery of the down-to-earth historical explanations of why such patterns emerged and why large groups of people respond to them in such different ways.

To struggle against each of these problems means that you think alternatives are possible. War, mass starvation, death from disease, global environmental devastation—maybe these are aspects of life that have always been and always will be with us. Maybe they reflect unchangeable human nature. Maybe they reflect the Will of God. Maybe they are part of an unstoppable process of evolution. Once you start trying to change these patterns, even in the most direct and down-to-earth ways, you are acting on a different conviction. You are saying, in your own way, that humanity's future is not completely predetermined. Collectively, human beings have the ability to shape different destinies for themselves.

You are also saying that some futures are better than others. We humans face strategic choices. A world without hunger, disease, poverty, war, environmental degradation, the subordination of women and gays, and wars fought in the name of nations and religions would be better than our present-day world. To be a leftist means thinking that human beings could organize themselves in such a way that these evils would be at least diminished if not ultimately eliminated. To be a leftist means throwing oneself into the problems of the present in the gamble that these problems are not just eternal aspects of the human condition.

The sociologist Zygmunt Bauman has developed these simple insights into a brilliant distillation of the project of the left, which in most recent human history has gone under the name of "socialism." (I'll get back to that word, which I use in its broadest possible sense, later.) Bauman sees socialism as a kind of "utopianism." As soon as many leftists hear that word, their backs go up. Isn't that just what their enemies have always said—that the left is full of idealistic daydreamers, people clinging to a childish dream of "heaven on earth"? But Bauman doesn't mean that kind of "utopianism." What he means is that leftists typically put forward visions of the future that are radically different from the conditions of present-day reality. "Utopias" in this sense are aspects of culture in which "possible extrapolations of the present are explored." They are, in a sense, thought-experiments in living otherwise.

In general, Bauman says, leftists are more inclined to realism than to romanticism. When they draw upon their experiences in solving particular issues, they have been surprisingly down-to-earth. When leftists use utopias, they are doing so as a technique to "help to lay bare and make conspicuous the major divisions of interest within a society." Their utopias are present-day expressions of the "other world" that human collective action might make possible. Although utopias generally address society as a whole—"here's a future that would be good for all of us"—they actually work to reveal that society is made up of very different groups with radically different interests.

"In other words," writes Bauman, "utopias relativise the future into a bundle of class-committed solutions, and dispel the conservative illusion that one and only one thread leads on from the present." Against the many people who say, of a given social problem, "Well, that's just human nature" or "That's just the way things have always been" or "The poor ye have always with you," concrete utopias suggest that things that seem to be just "natural" parts of life are actually the outcome of history and politics—of the forces and choices people made, perhaps many generations ago, that still shape our world today. Utopias "portray the future as a set of competing projects, and thereby reveal the role of human volition and concerted effort in shaping and bringing it about."[5]

No law in the universe lays down that some Torontonians and Montrealers live in cardboard boxes and others in 5,000-square-foot houses equipped with plasma-screen television sets and hot tubs. No inescapable logic rules that many Aboriginal Canadians in the north are required to have a life expectancy far lower than that of Euro-Canadians in the south.

These are matters of *history* and *politics*. Consequently, they are within the limits that every one of us inherits from human choices made in the past.

In considering the HIV/AIDS pandemic, for example, critics might argue that it is "utopian" to think that the population of the world could mobilize its resources to save a majority of the estimated forty-two million people living with the disease. After all, to date, heavy evidence indicates that the most powerful, rich, and priestly people in the world are against making that happen. Yet other conflicting indications also exist. There is Stephen Lewis, for example, the one-man left-wing crusade for justice for Africa. There is the 1980s legacy of brave struggle on the part of the gay communities—historically among the most despised and outcast minorities in North American society—fighting for dear life against historic patterns of indifference and prejudice, much of it found in the conventional left. Most impressively, there is emergent grassroots activism in Africa itself, with some notable victories in some states. In North America's gay communities in the 1980s huge victories were won when an oppressed community took up a life-and-death struggle and linked it to a more general vision of freedom. We can project from the reality of corporate greed, indifference to the poor, and religious and official prejudice and inhumanity; or we can project from a reality of successful grassroots activism that has already changed lives from San Francisco to South Africa.

With global warming, for example, it is certainly possible to project into the future the continuance of current practices, which might quite possibly spell the end of human life on the planet. These practices are deeply rooted in how most Westerners, living in the world's dominant capitalist economies, make their living. A realistic "utopian" projection of a more balanced, long-term approach begins with a scientific understanding of biology, physics, and chemistry, with explorations of the Earth's atmosphere, with an understanding that human beings, as animals, confront real limits to what they can or should do if they want to survive on this planet. Neither "projection" is unscientific, but the second, Bauman would say, is an example of a "concrete utopia." Just to point out that human beings have a collective interest in survival that global capitalism may be placing at risk is to "portray the future as a set of competing projects."

To be a leftist, then, means an immersion in urgent day-by-day struggles and a willingness to see the connections linking them together. But it also means introducing into the world a vision of the future and producing a logical program for its realization. It means defending that vision against constant hostility. Projecting a "utopia" into the present means understanding all the forces—such as those organized by class, gender, race, sexual orientation, nationality—that are likely to fight against it, even if the utopia in question is just a modest proposal for cleaner air that would bring even the left's enemies healthier and longer lives.

When Karl Marx, in the posthumously published third volume of *Capital*, considered this concept of the "real utopia," he used the term "realm of freedom." Marx was an ardent democrat, back when democracy was a far-fetched and disreputable revolutionary idea. He despised the world of privilege and elitism and scorned liberals who talked non-stop about the rights of individuals without realizing that none of these individuals and none of their "inalienable" rights could exist apart from society. Today Marx and the Marxists are often depicted as crackpots urging their followers into a mad "lovers' leap" into an unknown future. (And many of the twentieth-century regimes supposedly based on Marx's ideas were guilty as charged.) But when you actually read Marx, you will find the opposite message. Marx spent a lifetime reasoning otherwise. His message to people who needed to believe without evidence and without doing the hard work of analysis was in accord with his own personal motto: "Doubt everything."[6]

Marx fully described his "real utopia" in his masterpiece, *Capital*, and—if you can get past some of his dated Victorian expressions—his words resonate today.

> The realm of freedom really begins only where labour determined by necessity and external expediency ends; it lies by its very nature beyond the sphere of material production proper. Just as the savage must wrestle with nature to satisfy his needs, to maintain and reproduce his life, so must civilized man, and he must do so in all forms of society and under all modes of production. This realm of natural necessity expands with his development, because his needs do too; but the productive forces to satisfy these expand at the same time. Freedom, in this sphere, can consist only in this, that socialized man, the associated producers, govern the human metabolism with nature in a rational way, bringing it under their collective control instead of being dominated by it as a blind power; accomplishing it with

> the least expenditure of energy and in conditions most worthy and appropriate for their human nature. But this always remains a realm of necessity. The true realm of freedom, the development of human powers as an end in itself, begins beyond it, though it can only flourish with this realm of necessity as its basis.[7]

Like so much in Marx, it is a passage that you could spend a lifetime pondering. Those who have written about it disagree with each other. I see in it an approach very similar to the one described by Bauman: it is possible to live otherwise, but keep your feet on the ground. In any imaginable future there will be fields to be ploughed, dishes to be washed, diapers to be changed, folks to look after. Yet even as we carry out all the mundane tasks that keep body and soul together, we can still live otherwise. Even as we do the things we need to do to survive, we can manage things collectively more rationally than we now do. We can invest the everyday world with meaning and purpose. But *alongside* that realm of necessity—notice, Marx says "beyond" but not "above"—there begins another realm, the "true realm of freedom." In that realm the development of human creativity—building relationships, making music or drawing pictures, doing philosophy, birding, quilting, playing hockey—is an end in itself.

Marx is not talking about a "dualistic vision," in the same way that some Christians view heaven as the complete opposite of a sinful and troubled Earth. He is talking about an Earth transformed. The realm of freedom is not removed from the realm of necessity—it couldn't exist without it—but it is also not the same thing. In this realm of freedom, there is a capacity to create that can only emerge when people feel prosperous and comfortable and at home in providing for themselves and those they love. It is the vision of a utopian, but a utopian with dirt under the fingernails.

This passage has had a long underground life. In Latin America, for example, it inspired a whole tradition of reading Christ's gospel as a call to social revolution. It has also appealed to environmental activists trying to transcend long-standing exploitive approaches to nature, because the "rational management" of a metabolism is a far cry from a one-way strategy of corporate dominance. Instead of seeing the "realm of freedom" as a socialist version of the bland Christian heaven—with white-coated scientists and a gleaming Starship Enterprise taking the place of sexless celestial choirs and pearly gates—Marx sees it more as an unfolding here-and-now process, a freeing of human possibilities stifled prematurely or destroyed altogether in our modern world. This is a Marx, for example, that I can imagine celebrating both the necessity to struggle against HIV/AIDS and the project of free sexual expression that lay historically at the heart of the major community that began this struggle in North America; and savouring the prospect of the hours of hard labour, and the human solidarities, that are entailed in the struggle against global warming.[8]

In the everyday world of the corporate twenty-first century, "necessity" and "freedom" confront each other as opposites. Many of us work so hard for those weekends off, when we can finally be ourselves, listen to music, get outdoors, or simply enjoy each other's company—when we can find the time to do so after completing the other mundane tasks of life that more and more seem to fill up the weekends. But weekends would not exist without our working weeks; and times at work can also be filled with pockets of freedom and spontaneity. The hard collective work of wiring a hospital building, for instance, can be a time of fun, solidarity, excitement, and creativity, and if it isn't so, it could be made so. In fact, "freedom and necessity" aren't neatly separated opposites. You can't have one without the other. Human beings collectively can expand the "realm of freedom" through a more rational management of the "realm of necessity." Instead of working for the weekend, we can experience both our workweeks and our leisurely weekends with a sense of participating in an important human project, as part of a caring and generous human community. Marx's projection of a human potential for creativity makes us look twice at the everyday world. Most of all, he makes us realize that this everyday world is not just a "thing" but a process and a problem, which can be addressed only by working to understand it.

Marx was the most brilliant and influential of all the "concrete utopians." For more than a century—the first significant Canadian reprint from Marx dates from the 1870s—Canadian socialists have been wrestling with his legacy. They almost always claim rights to the "one true Marx," although the historian can't help but notice that this one true Marx changes from one age to the next, in ways that would most likely have amused the actual human being named Karl Marx (b.1818–d.1883). It is as if his writings have worked like a complicated cultural time-release capsule: they release different energies and insights in different periods. "Marx" has been refuted countless times, and decisively so—anti-leftists especially must have hoped—with the fall of the Soviet Union in 1989; yet another "Marx" seems to be emerging in the twenty-first century. This time Marx is at the nucleus of the critique of a process of economic globalization that is having an impact on the entire human species.

Much of the existing literature on the place of Marx in Canadian left history is frustrating and, at times, simply wrong. The many liberals who have written histories of socialism contentedly apply the formula Marxism = Communism = Stalinism, reserve the label of Marxist for a few tendencies and parties, and convey the impression that Marx (and European socialist thought more generally) has been of marginal concern for most Canadian socialists. Actually, it is easy to show the opposite. Marx has been read intensively by every major school and contingent of Canadian leftists, from the 1890s to today. The reason for the confusion is that, since about the late 1940s, the sense of what "Marx" means has been frozen into a specific set of ideas, associated with a particular set of texts. If you start to think of Marx not as three or four set-in-stone theories, but as a dynamic and changing cultural code, which has interacted differently with the societies it has encountered over time, you start to see Marx more as a process than as a simple set of texts. Since the actual writer's death in 1883, the term Marx has referred not just to his writings (many of which were not generally accessible until the 1970s), and not just to his political program—but also to the complicated and surprising ways in which this time-release capsule has interacted with succeeding generations. Marx periodically emerges and re-emerges, sometimes bearing hitherto-unavailable texts, critiquing a previous Marx. It is quite possible, and these days very likely, to conceive of living and reasoning otherwise without being a "Marxist." It is hard to imagine doing so without having at least some sort of dialogue with "Marx"—this decades-long process through which so many past generations have struggled to reason and to live otherwise.

Entire generations of both socialists and anti-socialists have thought they had found in Marx an "economic determinist" who provided iron-clad laws of social development. Others found in the young Marx a radically voluntarist "revolutionary humanist" with a vision of a true human essence imprisoned in the material world. Conflicts between essence and construction, agency and structure, freedom and fate—conflicts that in other contexts are identified with radically different schools and thinkers—are in Marx fought out in the same texts, often in the same paragraphs and even within the same sentence. Marx's most influential single text, *Capital: A Critique of Political Economy*, is a "scientific" text that "critiques"—on political, logical, and ethical grounds—the very object it constructs. (A parallel from natural science might be something like *Symbiosis: A Critique of Biological Science.*) A tension between "structure" and "agency" is built right into the very title of this famous book. Marx wanted to found the realm of freedom on the most rigorous understanding of the massive network of relations that make us unfree so that our critique of those relations can be all the more effective.[9] As the Sardinian thinker and activist Antonio Gramsci so nicely put it:

> Karl Marx is not, for us, the infant whimpering in the cradle or the bearded man who frightens priests. . . . He is an individual moment in the anxious search that humanity has been conducting for centuries to acquire consciousness of its being and its becoming, to grasp the mysterious rhythm of history and disperse the mystery, to be stronger in its thinking and to act better. He is a necessary and integral part of our spirit, which would not be what it is if he had not lived, had not thought, had not sent sparks of light flying from the collision with his passions and his ideas, his sufferings and his ideals.[10]

In the conversation with "Marx" that means most to me, the "realm of freedom" is not just a way of talking about some distant utopia. It is a way of understanding and extending the democratic spaces that we are able to experience in the daily world. In the everyday world of capitalism, small realms of freedom can be carved out of working lives—spaces and times in which individuals and groups can find time to think about the world and their places in it. At other times everyday realms of freedom become much larger and the daily rhythms of life are suspended. Mind-transforming questions are asked. Why should workers not receive the full value of the commodities they produce? Why should people starve on Third World streets when there is enough food in the world to feed everyone? Why should Aboriginal peoples be treated like second-class citizens in their own country? Why should parliament be dominated by men? Why should so many women have to flee their homes and find refuge in shelters?

Why should gay men be bashed in back alleys and pilloried from the pulpit? Why should the new regimes of world trade tyrannize and impoverish much of the world?

Most of us have our moments of freedom when we feel as though we are more truly at home with the world, and at those moments large groups of people also share this feeling. A core part of these realms of freedom is the freedom to criticize the everyday world and to project alternative worlds into the future. In these and other anticipations of the realm of freedom, each specific to its time and all of them an anticipation of an authentic liberation, radicals and socialists have found their own social spaces and their own spaces in time. They have drawn upon the past to draw an imagined future closer. They have created social and intellectual spaces in which isolated individuals can see themselves as part of a much bigger story.

Socialist realms of freedom do not refer to science-fiction realms of abstract possibility. As Gramsci dryly observes in the classic *Prison Notebooks*—and here the echoes of Marx's earlier position are clear:

> Possibility is not reality: but it is in itself a [kind of] reality. Whether a man can or cannot do a thing has its importance in evaluating what is done in reality. Possibility means 'freedom.' [And that] measure of freedom enters into the concept of man. That objective possibilities exist for people not to die of hunger, and that people do die of hunger has its importance, or so one would have thought. But the existence of 'objective' conditions, of possibilities or of freedom is not yet enough: it is necessary to

> 'know' them, and know how to use them. And to want to use them.[11]

Like Bauman, Gramsci is talking about using a set of *objective possibilities* as a way of awakening people in the present and distinguishing friends from foes. To be a leftist is to use the possibility, the objective possibility, of living otherwise. It means building a sense of possibility into the very concept we hold of ourselves—of "knowing" it at a deep level—and understanding our context within a historical process bigger than we are. Knowing what this living otherwise entails means struggling to make the possibility a reality. We can abstractly imagine a world in which the lines of power and wealth are drawn very differently. Over time, if our projection is in fact something possible within a feasible world and not simply a "candy mountain" fantasy, it can become a kind of reality, as more and more people mobilize around it. People can only come to really "know" this possibility, in the full sense, by trying to make it happen; and making it happen means finding others who share the conviction that the possibility is there.

Take, for example, the sense of weary alienation experienced by many North Americans in travelling along congested stretches of fast-food restaurants, muffler shops, malls, and monster big box stores that lock in our cities. We might simply gripe or make snide jokes about them. We might vow to frequent only family-owned eateries or shop at small independent stores in the downtown core—if we can find any. We might resolve only to buy from our local organic farmer and boycott all branded merchandise. These kinds of personal decisions capture an authentic, resistant vision of an "otherwise." They create small spaces of personal critique and freedom, outside that manipulative and ugly commercialism that we might want to avoid. No discerning leftist should ridicule such small-scale acts of resistance, but neither should he or she be content with them. Isolated and dispersed across the social landscape, such little acts of freedom are vulnerable and short-lived. The "freedom" is confined to one person, one family, one moment, and it is often purchased through the "unfreedom" of others. The "realm of freedom" that the left, and the left alone, can act upon is one open to the vast majority of humankind. It might begin with small collective acts—such as "no shopping" days or local campaigns to stop the spread of Wal-Marts—but to be truly "of the left," it must connect these acts with a larger strategy, a more inclusive storyline. It must see every such struggle as a partial answer to a much bigger question, to which it contributes part of the answer: "How can we live differently?" What possibilities can we use to turn the little "measures" of freedom available to a few into much bigger realms of freedom open to the many? How can our small acts of resistance snowball into a system-changing social movement?

With this kind of question in mind, we can see in the grey shadowy details of the history of the Canadian left since 1890 the coherent shapes of the past possibilities that people tried to take up in order to live otherwise. Living in an often hostile individualistic social and political order—one that since the 1840s was increasingly well-fortified against dissenting opinions and that treated "democracy" first as a term of abuse and then as an "optional extra"—socialists were able to carve out limited realms of freedom, where they could, for a time, develop their alternatives. In some places and in some times, these realms of freedom—freedom from commodities, from necessity, freedom to self-expression, to enjoyment—attained a physical presence in parties and neighbourhoods and movements.

In these little realms of freedom it was possible to speak and act with a freedom generally reserved for the elite. With creativity and ingenuity, in the time remaining after work, left-wing men and women created spaces and traditions and even specialized bodies of concepts. They created a succession of realms of freedom in the interstices of everyday necessity. At the core of the set of objective possibilities that the Canadian left has characteristically defended is an ideal of a rational, just democracy.

TWO

Redefining the Left

THOUSANDS OF BOOKS and articles have been published, and theses written, about the Canadian left. This small book could not have been written without them. Just a few of the "must-read" titles appear in the endnotes here. This is a literature well worth getting to know. It is full of fascinating people and important debates.

It is also one that needs a major conceptual overhaul. Many of these works come with their own political agendas. They often serve up a potent brew of sectarianism and sentimentality. Sectarianism: *our tradition* has the goods, and every other approach to the left is mired in error and illusion. *Here* we have the truth. *There* you find the erroneous others. Sentimentality: *our heroes* were never complicated, cowardly or inconsistent.

Lately the agenda has often been different. Now, especially outside Canada, when many academics write about the left, they write tragic narratives. Big hopes are repeatedly betrayed. Bright young idealists turn into middle-aged bureaucrats with mortgages, car payments, and teeth as yellow as their old copies of

Monthly Review. Promising movements become party machines. In recent years, and especially after the collapse of the Soviet Union in 1989, the common tone of academic literature has been impatience and disillusionment. The entire left has been written off as the dead, unlamented pipe dream of the twentieth century. Post-1989, post-1995, and post-9/11, an intense mood of disillusionment with all-encompassing plans of "social improvement" has taken hold.[1]

Neo-liberals, following the lead of their master thinkers F.A. Hayek and Milton Friedman, argue that any attempt to impose a plan upon free markets means a "road to serfdom." They oppose any interference with the most precious tool that humanity has perfected to generate knowledge about its true wants and potentialities—the free, unregulated market. The analytically distinct if politically often identical neoconservatives base their equally strenuous anti-leftism on an adherence to the hierarchies that twentieth-century leftists kept calling into question: of men over women, normal over deviant, and God-fearing over irreligious. Together, and in various combinations, these forces of the "new right" have attained extraordinary cultural power in North America. They have seemingly moved into an unrivalled position to roll back what remains of the welfare state and the scientific enlightenment. Their influence has extended deep into the academy. They have succeeded in turning into a strange and frightening proposition any notion of a "realm of freedom" that diverges from the consumer's freedom to choose between Wal-Mart or Canadian Tire. We appear to be confronting a choice between locking ourselves away with a pure but narrow and self-serving concept of the "true history" of the left or writing off the entire idea as a totalitarian nightmare from which we are now awakening.

This book refuses both options. It has a different agenda. Contrary to the sectarian literature, it argues that it is possible to write *generally* about the left—in ways that allow its many thinkers and activists their place around the table, giving them a fair chance to have their "realms of freedom" remembered with accuracy and critiqued with respect. Contrary to contemporary right-wing literature, this books agrees with Gramsci that post-capitalist possibilities are still a kind of reality that contemporary crises (particularly the looming environmental catastrophe) will make more "objective" and pressing in our everyday life—even if it is often difficult to know exactly how to use those possibilities effectively. One way of getting to know something about our present possibilities is to develop a better understanding of how people in the past tried to construct and extend their own realms of freedom. What worked? What failed? What lives on? Meaningful answers to questions like that need more patience and time than either left-wing or right-wing sectarians generally allow. My sense of how to reach accurate and politically interesting answers from the history of the left is that we need to sit down and listen as attentively as we can to the leftists of the past, struggling with all our might to place their work in context. We need to balance our sympathy with their ends with a frank critique of many of their means. This book sets out in very preliminary outline what some of the principles of such an inquiry would be. It remains for other books, written by many hands in addition to my own, to realize the fullness of the inquiry's agenda.

The most obvious initial hurdle to any such project is that of providing initial definitions. The "left" is by no means a self-evident category. The term comes to us from the French Revolution and the French Constituent Assembly of 1789 to 1791, which was divided on the question of the king's remaining powers. Those who wanted to build an order radically different from the monarchy took to sitting to the left side of the chamber (as viewed from the president's seat). Conservatives sat on the right. Gradually "the left" came to be the name of those who wanted to abolish the king's veto power, to achieve a more democratic franchise. From the beginning, then, "the left" has always been a relational and contextual term for those pushing for radical democracy. Following Geoff Eley, we can define this left concept of democracy quite narrowly and minimally: "It requires at least the following: free, universal, secret, adult, and equal suffrage; the classic civil freedoms of speech, conscience, assembly, association, and the press; and freedom from arrest without trial."[2] Or we can define democracy more broadly and expansively: a state of civil society in which equal empowerment governs not only formal politics but also economic decision-making. In this *social* conception of democracy, the formal civil liberties still cherished by some liberals are all preserved. What's different is that attention is also paid to the human networks within which such individual liberties can actually flourish. In either case, the "narrow" case or the "broad" case, democracy, as we shall see, belongs to the left.[3]

For more than a century most leftists in Canada would also have defined themselves as "socialists."[4] This is a fighting word. For leftists it has traditionally been used to define who is "one of us," who is "one of them," and "who is pretending to be one of us, but is really one of them." In this well-entrenched approach, "socialism" is very much an "essence," a sort of timeless core of conviction, whose inner presence is proved by special outward signs: mastery of certain texts, participation in defining movements, identification with particular parties. In this essentialist mode, to re-experience the historical left is to enter an irresolvable debate about who was *really* a socialist. For some, Canadian socialism simply means identification with the historic mainstream tradition—which starts with the Co-operative Commonwealth Federation (CCF) (fd.1932–33) and extends to the New Democratic Party (NDP) (fd.1961). For others, this mainstream tradition stands not for socialism but for *social democracy*, the watered-down corruption of the true, original vision. For some, the real Canadian party of "socialism" was the Communist Party of Canada (CPC), which started underground in Canada in 1921, went above ground (as the Workers' Party) in 1922, and went through much of the 1940s as the Labor Progressive Party. For others this tradition stands not for socialism but for *authoritarian communism*. For some, especially in Quebec, there is no *Canadian* socialism, because the only true socialists were to be found in revolutionary groups whose reason for being was the revolutionary overthrow of the Canadian state. For others, there is no Canadian socialism because socialism is a revolutionary world-process in which Canada has no particular significance. Such battles over essential definition are characteristically unwinnable because the arguments brought forward usually involve no testable propositions founded in logic and evidence. They will probably go on as long as Canadian leftists draw breath.

Here I propose an alternative to socialism-as-essence. Most people can agree on a ballpark definition that covers what most Canadians have taken the term to mean (even as they disagree with each other over its application). In tracing the nineteenth-century history of the word the British thinker Raymond Williams shows that "social," from which "socialism" emerged, started off with two senses. The first was just a "descriptive term for society" as a "system of common life." The second was a more emphatic term that was explicitly contrasted with "individual" and "individualist" theories of society. A popular use of the first sense was the idea of developing, extending, and shoring up such values as political freedom and formal equality among different individuals and groups. A popular use of the second sense was that truly social reforms were opposed to individualist forms of society. Such reforms would only be significant if a society based on private property was replaced by "one based on *social* ownership and control."[5]

Socialist thought, especially in the West, has often combined these two senses. Socialists are those who take individual freedoms so seriously that they want to extend them as equally as possible to everyone. They want to apply principles of individual freedom to economic and social life in general and not just to the narrow world of formal politics. They see the "social" as a meaningful, desirable complement to—not a substitute for—the "individualistic." They think of society as made up not of atomized competitive individuals but of human beings bonded to each other by ties of common interest and shared values.

Along these lines the British writer Margaret Cole usefully defined "socialism" as a threefold doctrine: "(1) the belief that any society founded on large-scale private ownership is unjust; (2) the conviction that a more equitable form of society can be established, one that will contribute to the moral and material improvement of humankind; and (3) the idea that social revolution is imperative" (with significant debate regarding whether such revolution entails violence or gradual but thoroughgoing reform).[6] On the first point, socialists have generally been critical of social and economic inequality because they contend that the enrichment of the few occurs at the expense of the many. They are critical of the planlessness of capitalism, a way of life capable of producing anything except a plausible moral and political rationale for its own existence. On the second point, socialists think that some outcomes are better than others—that, for instance, a future in which most human beings at birth face roughly similar chances of long and healthy lives is preferable to one in which some people eke out an existence until they are twelve months old and others enjoy lives eighty times that long.

On the third point, leftists believe that far-ranging changes are necessary to the political and economic order in order to attain these preferable outcomes. Some consistently argue that reforming the existing political and economic system means that it will gradually be transformed into a system that produces these results. Others argue that the private property in production should be overthrown by direct action in a rapid transition to the socialist alternative. Most leftists at most times in Canada have located themselves on a continuum somewhere in between these poles—generally in favour of reforms that force the entire system to change or of revolutions that unfold over a much longer period of time.

We can add to this three-part understanding of socialism a fourth point drawn from Frederick Engels and Karl Marx's *Communist Manifesto*, possibly the most widely printed book, apart from the Bible, in human history, which its principal author (Marx) dashed off in several weeks from late 1847 to early 1848. The *Manifesto* maintained that socialism is not just an *ideal* but something *actually emerging*, a "set of objective possibilities," in the actual social and economic world around us. We can, as Antonio Gramsci said, *use* these possibilities. Marx and his friend and intellectual companion Engels considered the "socialism" of their day a stuffy, middle-class movement compared with their own radical "communist" alternative. Yet their *Manifesto* won most of its renown as a text in the large social-democratic parties organized throughout Europe in the last quarter of the nineteenth century. Not only, said Marx, is it possible to "live otherwise," but also because capitalism has changed traditional society beyond recognition—"all that is solid melts into air," in *The Communist Manifesto*'s famous remark—it is very possible that working people will be required to do so. They will, like the bourgeoisie before them, seize control of production and save their own lives from the poverty and degradation that the system has forced upon them. Marx believed that the dialectic itself—the great patterns of contradiction and conflict that he was convinced could be found in history—had created an immense opportunity for revolutionary change. A great insight in the *Manifesto*, which runs through all of the work of Marx, is that the more the capitalists succeeded in transforming the world, the more they risked undermining their own existence. They were like the sorcerer's apprentice, summoning up incredible powers of production and social change that they could only pretend to understand.[7]

Herein lies much of the difficulty in calling some people Marxists and then implying that they, alone, are the essential socialists. Much of what Marx had to say in *The Communist Manifesto*, *The Civil War in France*, and *Capital* would enter the common language of the left. Indeed, many of his conceptual tools would become part of the tool kit of most interpreters of modern society. Not everyone who uses these tools would agree to be called a Marxist. (Marx himself on one occasion objected to being called a Marxist.) What is more often meant when the word Marxist is applied, either as a blessing or a curse, is a much more specific political strategy—the strategy of a professional revolutionary vanguard as, for instance, developed by Lenin in *What Is to Be Done?* and other texts. Many writings assume that "Marxist" denotes a static, essential identity, and they then take up a stance, whether pro or more conventionally (in the Canadian case) con. Thanks largely to the Cold War, so entrenched has a reading of the "anti-democratic" Marx become that, when some students read *The Civil War in France*, with its warm words of praise for grassroots participatory democracy, they simply can't imagine that Marx wrote them.

In the early twenty-first century, when the very idea of the left is under siege, it seems far too late for these polemics. Because essentialism closes us off from the logical and empirical consideration of historical evidence, the boiling-down procedures it gives us—"who was really the Marxist?"—guarantee the endless repetition of irresolvable past debates. These debates will pay off richly only for those who have a deep psychological need to be absolutely in the right. They meet uncertainty with a deeply reassuring sense of an absolute truth outside history and politics. They produce a strongly conservative sense of solid ground when reality is in flux. In truth, such debates guarantee the perpetuation of the political marginality that is one of the harder truths we have to confront about the contemporary left worldwide. The primary commitments of the left are to freedom and solidarity. Essentialism is a way of foreclosing the possibility of freedom. It offers us the illusion of a stable core, and it also subverts the possibility of solidarity. It invites us to imagine ourselves as being infinitely superior to those to whom we speak or about whom we write. It creates an imaginary space of pure authority from which we can survey the world around us. In both ways, it insulates us from the very modernity that leftists are obliged to transform, as best they can, into a realm of freedom.

If the realm of freedom we imagine is "not a reality, but a kind of reality," as Gramsci put it, an everyday sphere in which growing numbers of people can "know" and "use" objective possibilities for living otherwise—if that is what we mean by a realm of freedom, then the old, clinging, insecure habits of essentialism have to be transcended. They arrive as so much left luggage from the twentieth century. Valuable as many of the sectarian and sentimental books will always be as sources of information and inspiration, it feels too late in the early twenty-first century to content ourselves with this form of historical memory. We live in an intensely right-wing era in which *The Communist Manifesto*'s assumption that the system is automatically generating its own gravediggers, and that the abolition of the market will usher in an age of human happiness, does not ring as exactly true for us as it did for Marx in 1848. Replaying scenes of old factional debates and writing with a false certainty about being the defenders of the one correct Marxist side in all of them now seem more like ways of denying rather than of confronting the changing political realities of our own time. The books generated with this approach often seem to be written to police the frontiers of a small, embattled, cultish tradition and not to probe the ways in which the tradition can be understood and then extended in a more rigorous and yet sympathetic sense. Many of the texts seem like ethically dubious exercises in hubris—wordy demonstrations of a superior writer's ownership of a small plot of theory and history. They work like the property-holder's little fences: holding competitors and the wilderness at bay and staking a small claim to possession of the genuine thing.

Anybody who shares four key insights—that is, into capitalism's injustice, the possibility of equitable democratic alternatives, the need for social transformation, and the real-world development of the preconditions of this social transformation in the actual world around us—can be called a leftist. In Canada, most people committed to an "objective set of possibilities" based on grassroots democracy have been called socialists. Yet the relationship between socialism and the left's wider project of democracy is complex. The "left" struggling for the enhancement of democracy has always been larger than socialism. "Socialists," says Geoff Eley in his brilliant book *Forging Democracy*, "never carried their goals alone." Some have adopted the label "communist" and joined vanguard parties; others have adopted the name "anarchist" and, especially in recent years, have built an impressive network of countercultural places, groups, and Internet sites; and there are today many other names.[8]

The traditional approach invites us to see each one of these names as labels for separate species that compete with other species in a struggle of the ideologically fittest to survive in the dog-eat-dog world of political warfare. If, for instance, you identify imaginatively with the Communist Party and differentiate its "Marxist" followers from "social democrats"—not a common viewpoint in the general population, but fashionable with many academic labour historians—the governing assumption is that a Communist was a Communist was a Communist: in 1921, 1935, 1956, or 1989. If you identify with the CCF-NDP—a much more common viewpoint in the general population, with some support in the academy—you might argue that the "democratic left" was much the same in 1921, 1932, 1948, and 1968, and always at war with the Communists. Once in play, these categories become more and more reified: Marxists and social democrats (and so on) fight on through the ages. The names of the individuals change; the battles remain the same.

Writing history in this way does have its strengths, and applied to fairly short periods of time, and well-defined bodies of people, a strategy of clearly labelling parties and positions makes a lot of sense. If we look, for example, at the mid-1930s, the sharp differences between those identifying themselves as Communists and those calling themselves CCFers are obvious. There is room for many more histories of the left's parties and people, and no doubt a good number of them will incorporate the assumption that party *x* and individual *y* were, in contrast to all other competitors, "of the essence" of the true Canadian left.

Yet there is also a good argument for writing history another way. If you think of the first approach as a vertical approach that traces lines of descent like roots and branches through the past, this second approach is a horizontal approach that looks at how leftists in a given period shared many things. Or if you want to think in terms of "species," the first approach invites you to think of species of leftists as fixed essences: a social democrat is a social democrat. The second approach invites you to agree with Charles Darwin (and with Marx) that species are mutable and not fixed, that they change in a complex dialectic with their surroundings and that they may influence each other. This approach looks at all the people and parties who made up a given period in the history of the left. It assumes that each period, in complex ways, makes its own practice of leftism; that leftists in each period invent distinctive conceptual systems through which they grasp the world. They construct their own dialect of the general language of socialism. Some resist the new dialect, some refuse to learn it, and some stop "speaking socialism" altogether—but, for most people on the left, the new dialect works better than the old one. Even those who don't share the core assumptions of those who have initiated the new way of speaking socialism may well find themselves having to share their words, if they want to make sense to their contemporaries and speak to the big issues of their day. Each group of leftists, defined by time, place, demography, types of institutions, and leading ideas, creates a kind of experiment in "living otherwise." If today we want to try any such experiment ourselves, we can only profit from studying their past efforts with as open a mind as possible.

THE PATHS TO SOCIALISM

The break with older traditions of left history-writing goes beyond a new strategy for looking at the relationships between groups to encompass a broader conception of how these groups came into being in the first place—a new conception of the "origin" of left species, so to speak. Drawing fairly directly from the vision of history articulated in *The Communist Manifesto*, many writers have implicitly suggested not only that the histories of socialism and of the working class have intertwined but also that the history of socialism is merely an element in the bigger story of the making of the working class.

In the twentieth century thousands of Canadian industrial workers rallied to the left. In Nova Scotia, Alberta, and British Columbia, coal miners in particular earned a reputation as ardent socialists. Across Canada there are places whose names will always resonate with people who want to live otherwise: Nanaimo, Crow's Nest Pass, Estevan, Winnipeg, Sudbury, Windsor, Oshawa, Spadina, Asbestos, Glace Bay. Sites of left memory one and all, because each was a site of working-class resistance. Why become a leftist? Because of exploitation at the point of production and the appropriation of surplus value by the capitalists; because of the exemplary role of other leftists in leading class struggles and extracting better hours, wages, and working conditions from the bosses.

We might call this the "proletarianization" model of leftism. It echoes the class-based analyses of many leftists in the nineteenth and early to mid-twentieth centuries. The left told itself that the industrial working class was growing year by year, while the increasingly redundant and desperate "middle strata" were being driven out of existence. Leftists often worked with a "linear model" of class-consciousness following industrial development. Yet in fact the pattern throughout the West has been infinitely more complicated than they allowed. Even in Britain the industrial proletariat did not become a majority of the population, and it is now contracting, not expanding. In many respects, as Eley remarks, the "unity" of the working class that socialists so firmly described and prescribed was an "idealized projection," an abstraction from "the disorderly and unevenly developing histories of industrialization in the nineteenth century, whose visible concentrations of laboring poor certainly impressed contemporaries but required sustained action before settling into a pattern."[9]

The opposite temptation has been to express frustration with workers for not becoming socialists, or voice disdain for the limited experiments they did contribute to in the Socialist, Communist, CCF, and New Democratic parties. The workers are called before the bar of history to answer for the specific biases (gender, race, and sexual orientation) of their leftism. The decline of "class" as a fashionable topic coincided with neo-liberalism's ascendancy to enormous influence inside and outside the academy. There are now no more working coal mines or steel mills, but a variety of new call centres, in even so historic a land of the left as industrial Cape Breton. Thus from both left and right come predictions of socialism's inevitable demise, often accompanied by disparagement of the achievements and future of the industrial working class.

The popular class-based model is overdue for rigorous discussion. Most working-class people in Canada did not become leftists. Many—perhaps most?—twentieth-century Canadians who became leftists were not from the working class. Even in legendary sites of struggle like the Vancouver Island and Nova Scotia coalfields, the socialists were, more often than not, in the minority. Individualistic liberalism, in all its guises, has always had a much larger working-class base in Canada than has socialism. Writing again and again of the Canadian working class as though it were (essentially, or "really") socialistic seems like an exercise in wishful thinking.

Reducing the history of Canadian leftism to the history of class is related to past habits of sectarianism and sentimentalism. If you think your politics superior to that of other leftists, the temptation is to see yourself as part of a process of social evolution that is deeper than theirs. No matter what the setbacks, you can fortify yourself with the thought that, eventually, your day will come. The result is a form of left "triumphalism" that allows you to feel superior to superficial souls who are unable to see that your leftism is being carried forward by the currents of history itself. *You* speak for the class that is making history; *they* speak for people bound for history's waste bin.

Still, there is a huge potential, and sometimes actual, overlap between the interests of workers as workers and any political project of the left. The left stands for, and makes a part of present reality, an egalitarian and democratic vision of a realm of freedom. The left also represents a critical approach to political economy. It generally maintains that capitalism intrinsically cannot dispense with labour-power, which it buys and sells like any other commodity. To "bid farewell to the proletariat" or celebrate "the end of the working class" is to demonstrate moral and empirical blind spots. Who makes the stuff that you and I need? Who sells it in stores? Who serves us in restaurants? Who is answering our phone calls in faraway places? Are they exploited in doing so? What would happen if they united and changed how things are made and distributed? How can we possibly imagine a better world without also imagining how people in it will make their living? To imagine that one could build a left that did not centrally address the economic and social demands of working-class people, that did not derive in some measure from the push to realize a concrete universal drive for equality, is to imagine something other than a recognizable socialism. Yet to mistake this potential for reality is to demonstrate an equally impressive blind spot. The history of socialism is related to and informed by working-class history—but the two are not, and never have been, one and the same.

Class-based radicalism, then, has sometimes led to the left in Canada, but so too have at least seven other paths. At specific times and in specific places these other paths were just as, and even more, important. In many areas we find diaspora leftisms. Such ethnically based radicalisms often overlapped, but cannot be equated, with the ones that emerged from the industrial working class. By some estimates, more than 90 per cent of the Communist Party membership in Canada in the late 1920s was made up of recently arrived Finns, Ukrainians, and Jews. Why did they become leftists? Partly because of class injustices at the point of production—as the orthodox Marxist will always insist—but also because of stories heard around the dinner table, the histories and values learned in the Finnish or Jewish Socialist Hall, or the news brought from crisis-prone decaying European empires, most prominently those of Russia and Austria. Here timing and context were everything, determining not just how strongly ethnic attachments were experienced, but also how emphatically that group articulated its politics.

The most ambitious human genome project is unlikely to find a genetic sequence that explains why so many Finns were radicals in Canada. Before 1914 many were émigrés not just from a brutal Russian Empire but also from a corner of it in which the social-democratic movement was far ahead of the rest of the continent. They congregated together in large populations in Northern Ontario and the West. Their language and customs set them apart, even as their experiences in lumber camps and mines united them with other workers. Treated like second-class subjects in Canada, they had every reason to organize and resist in Finnish ways, in the Finnish language, drawing upon Finnish legends and traditions.[10]

Another distinct path to the left, our third, was opened up by the country's complicated and perpetual three-part "national question." The first part—whether Canada should exist as an independent country—preoccupied many anglophone Canadians down to the 1980s. One powerful form of that brand of leftism took root in the Waffle faction of the relatively mainstream New Democratic Party. Even more striking was the response to the second part of the national question: whether Quebec should be seen as an integral part of Canada or as a conquered nation struggling to escape from the yoke of colonialism. The anglophone Canadian left started wondering about Quebec as early as 1902. When the Québécois themselves started asking the national question en masse in the 1960s, they often couched mass support for Quebec's independence in terms of achievement of a realm of freedom outside capitalist social relations. The third, Aboriginal part of the national question became a major issue for the left after the rise of a new First Nations activism in the 1960s. There is a huge potential overlap, not as yet fully realized, between, on the one hand, patterns of collective decision-making, respect for nature, non-capitalist community-based regimes of property, and implicitly non-liberal First Nations philosophies of history and, on the other, the outlook of a twenty-first-century post-colonial Canadian left, especially one that has actively embraced a philosophy and a politics based more upon listening than on lecturing.

Since the 1960s, because of this three-part national question, Canada's existence as a political community has never seemed based on anything like a certainty. What that means is that those who project radically different political futures, including socialists, are not so easily silenced by appeals to common-sense realism or unreflecting patriotism. Evicting the Parti Québécois from Quebec City, or the Assembly of First Nations from treaty negotiations, on the grounds of supposed "anti-Canadianism" are not realistic options, certainly not for leftists. A country in which so many basics remain undefined leaves ample room for realms of freedom in which all basics are open to rational questioning.[11]

A fourth path has often arisen from reflection and activism based on gender liberation movements. Socialists, initially almost all of them men, had been asking "the woman question" since the 1880s, but the "question" started to sound very different when many women themselves began asking it. Women's liberation (which flourished from, roughly, 1966 to 1990) generated a massive interest in the ideas of the left and created in Canada a socialist-feminist tradition that is unusual in terms of its theoretical cogency, organizational sophistication, and political influence. From the orthodox point of view that sees the history of socialism strictly in terms of proletarianization, many such left feminists were just building "new social movements" based on "personal politics"—not a socialist movement. From the perspective of a more inclusive leftism, socialist feminism meant that heterosexual male socialists were being asked to notice and act on the everyday acts of oppression and injustice that implicated themselves. From this socialist-feminist critique emerged a gay and lesbian radicalism that put all the conventional language of left politics, including that of socialist feminism itself, under critical scrutiny. The "objective possibility" of a future without gender and sexual oppression became the stuff of day-to-day left politics, extending from countless daily debates to the 2004 deliberations of the Supreme Court on same-sex marriage rights, a breakthrough that may well change the landscape of possibility for gays and lesbians in Europe as well as North America.[12]

A fifth much-travelled route to leftism in Canada begins with a spiritual awakening—meaning, for the majority, within Protestant and Catholic forms of Christianity. Radical historians are sharply divided when they come to talking about religion. Some hail the "Social Gospel" (which flourished, at least according to some accounts, from 1890 to 1939) as a massive challenge to conventional political assumptions. Given that many elements of capitalism are in tension, to put it mildly, with the letter and spirit of Christ's teachings as they are reported in the New Testament, Christians who take their religion seriously have had to wrestle with glaring contradictions. If they are truly committed to a gospel that takes the side of the poor, they feel uncomfortable in churches that have historically catered to the rich.

Many such Christians came to strikingly post-capitalist positions in the 1920s and 1930s, and they figured among the most renowned Canadian leftists of their generation. So too did a cohort of radical Catholics in Quebec; their post-1950s social activism and scepticism towards received tradition have continued to nurture an important, durable strand of activism and critique. Many left historians in both linguistic communities are uncomfortable, as secularists, when face-to-face with evidence suggesting the power of religion as a force for socialism. Yet many leftists in Canada have been believers, rooting resistance to capitalism in religious values.

In a broader sense Judeo-Christian assumptions are buried deep within the Marxist tradition itself, as both its enemies and liberation theologists have had no trouble in demonstrating. Whatever their substantial differences, both St. Paul and Karl Marx can be heard arguing that the free-standing "individual" at the heart of liberal political theory and economics is at best an incomplete and at worst a dangerous fiction. Nowadays a powerful and sophisticated critique of egoistic individualism emanates from Buddhism, one of North America's fastest-growing faith communities.[13]

Of growing significance in modern times is a sixth path, of intellectual inquiry. In the nineteenth century a gaping hole was opened in the classical liberal Protestant universe by the historical criticism of the Bible and by Darwinian theories of evolution. These placed a question mark on interpretations of history that emphasized God's direct intervention in human affairs. A common figure on the left has been the man or woman who identifies wholeheartedly with the scientific enlightenment and with the ideal of science as an inherently democratic, mind-opening activity. Scientists-cum-socialists, people who have arrived at a critique of capitalism on the grounds of its inherent irrationality, are common figures on the Canadian left. The contemporary environmental crisis has multiplied their numbers, and so too did the massive post-1945 expansion of post-secondary education.[14]

Seventh is the closely related path of global awareness. Directly influenced by movements in Great Britain and the United States, and since 1968 in France as well, the Canadian left has, almost by definition, been highly internationalist. In the second quarter of the twentieth century, tens of thousands enlisted in a Communist Party that saw itself as one regiment in a world revolutionary army. In the 1960s countless more were radicalized by protracted wars of decolonization in Algeria and Indochina and a seemingly endless Cold War between the Soviet Union and United States. Youth who went abroad to work in the developing world with non-governmental organizations were often profoundly changed—both by the glaring injustices of colonialism and by their subsequent attempts to apply lessons learned abroad to realities at home.

Newer forms of left globalism are less driven by such specific issues and more shaped by a general rejection of world economic and social inequalities and injustices. Major wars send thousands of people to the left, in short-term protest against the specifics of *this* war, but more lastingly because *all* wars come to be seen as the results of socio-economic imperatives. The looming international environmental crisis has probably radicalized as many Canadians today as did the economic crisis of the 1930s.[15]

In some instances leftists are those who have passed through experiences peculiar to their generations, which leads them down an eighth path to socialism. Whether "political generations" exist has been a matter of dispute since sociologist Karl Mannheim first introduced the concept in 1952. On the one hand it seems rather far-fetched to argue that the mere fact of being born at a certain time can explain why someone develops a certain stance towards the world. On the other hand there are undoubtedly whole periods in which people who share an age group also share many political attitudes. In modern life most of us pass through various institutions—schools, universities, armies, pension plans, homes for the elderly—in age-specific cohorts. Youth is a special time, when ways of seeing and categories of analysis are in flux. Perhaps the soldiers who fought in the Second World War formed the most solidly left-wing cohort in Canadian history. The spectre of a return to world war has haunted the three generations of Canadians who came into their own after 1945.[16] Patterns specific to generations might provide a useful means of explaining why, every twenty-five years or so, the left undergoes a major conceptual and organizational overhaul.

This last grouping reveals that the "eight paths to socialism" typology is an analytical device, not an empirical description. In any actual historical moment, as when young people are told to fight a war they did not choose and do not support, reconstructing the path to radicalism means paying attention to cross-currents and complications. Paths combine and intertwine. More crucially, they also often blend into each other, without one necessarily trumping all the others. Many people often start with one set of issues and over time come to emphasize others. For example, the turn-of-the-century Christian, appalled by the horrible suffering of overworked children in Montreal's unregulated sweatshops, might conclude her reflections by calling for more charity work among the poor. But once she went further, and tracked the reasons as to why some people were poor and others rich, why many fellow believers did not want to change and perhaps could not even see the problem, and why it was connected with a host of other problems—then she was setting out on the slippery socialist slope. Many workers, to give another example, may have first seen their socialism as a direct reflection of the class struggle and socialism essentially as an answer to the question, "How can workers fight for the value of the full product of their labour?" As time went on these workers often became self-taught intellectuals who found in Marxist economics and socialist politics new ways of understanding what they had experienced in the workplace. By the late 1920s, after the crest of the great working-class revolt of 1919–25, they might well still be persisting as socialist intellectuals, having been persuaded by a new view of history that the capitalist system was irrational and replaceable. Or a 1960s Quebec nationalist, angered by the linguistic arrogance of the anglophone elite in Montreal, might conclude his critique by joining an ethnically defined nationalist association. But after going further, tracking the historical roots of Quebec's oppression and linking it to the anti-capitalist decolonization struggles sweeping the world, he might well find himself arguing that Quebec's struggle only made sense if it were also a fight for a more all-inclusive socialist, anti-imperialist politics.[17]

Then again, if, for example, you are a middle-class university student worried about environmental planetary change, we might say that you're starting off on the sixth path. The spectres of the dying coral reefs off Belize, the ailing muskoxen of the Northwest Territories, or the smog-filled skies of Toronto trouble you. Why, morally or logically, should human beings do these things to their planet and their fellow human beings? Maybe that is where you will choose to end your journey—perplexed, passively awaiting the next bad environmental news item to come over the airwaves and Internet. But possibly you will want to go on. As you read more and more, you may start to develop a spiritual critique of the crisis. It will start to bother you, not only as an affront to rationality, but also as an attack on that delicate balance needed for any sense of wholeness and connection with the wider world. You may also start to connect the pattern with First Nations issues—because many of the environmental debates in Canada involve struggles between Aboriginal peoples and multinational corporations bent on using the entire planet as a "standing reserve" for capital. But what—you might start to wonder—is it about capitalism as a system that seems to compel it to accumulate and accumulate yet more? What is driving this process? Once you have reached that point, you have probably started to become self-consciously "of the left" and feel a certain interest in, and responsibility for, its history. Your leftism is as "solid" and as "real" as that of anyone else, even if you have never been down a coal mine or taken up arms with a revolutionary group in Latin America. From this point of view, becoming a leftist is not like acquiring street-fighting credentials, exhibiting a death-defying mastery of Marx's *Capital*, or defeating rivals in theoretical and political combat in the ritualized dialectical duels for which Marxist men have long been famous. It is more a life commitment to contribute to shared conversations and collective acts that hasten the day of a more generous democracy.

Paying attention to all of these eight paths seems to make more sense than focusing exclusively only on the first of them and treating it as a determination of "real leftism." A basic question that anyone on the left must ask is whether he or she has any chance of speaking to an audience larger than a small crowd of fellow-believers. All the successful left movements that have integrated these themes into something larger, a more system-challenging framework of activism and analysis, have taken care to maintain a healthy relationship with working-class Canadians and the labour movement that Canadians have painstakingly built. Canadian leftism cannot be seen as the passive reflection of the working class; yet if it arrogantly writes off the workers—which, to their credit, most Canadian leftists have never done—it misses one of its best opportunities to speak to a wider constituency. Leftism cannot be reduced to class; but without a sense of the class dimension of most social and economic issues, it is itself much reduced.

THREE

Liberal Order and the Shaping of Resistance

IN THE 1960S THE gifted political scientist Gad Horowitz speculated that the survival of the socialist idea on Canadian soil was connected to the country's status as a Tory "fragment" of Great Britain. Tendencies to organic conservatism in Britain (within the landed aristocracy and the church, for example) were brought to Canada, either directly or thanks to the Loyalists, that is, those who backed the losing side in the American Revolution and came as refugees to British North America. Thanks to the legacies of Loyalism and British Toryism, twentieth-century socialists found it easier to make the case for big state programs that went beyond U.S.-style liberal individualism. Horowitz coined the popular phrase "Red Tories," by which he meant Tories with a strong sense of "organic" community, one that distinguished them sharply from American laissez-faire liberals.

Horowitz's argument chimes with some evidence (it explains, for example, how some Saskatchewan farmers in the 1960s could simultaneously vote for the Conservatives federally and the socialists provincially). Yet, however brilliantly crafted, it has worked better as a way of legitimating the socialist legacy as an element within powerful elites in the country than it does as an overall explanation of the ebbs and flows of the history of the Canadian left. As a realistic depiction of Canadian left history, the Horowitz thesis falls short. Few correlations exist, for example, between areas of Loyalist settlement and socialist strength; British Columbia shows few traces of Red Toryism, yet since 1900 has displayed many indications of a substantial left base. It is not even at all clear whether most Loyalists were Tories in the sense that Horowitz requires. Most crucially, before the 1930s there was not much difference in the social policies of Canada and the United States. Horowitz's thesis seems to demand that "Canada" stands for a polity that is much more cohesive and corporative than that of the individualistic United States, yet when historians go back to the 1930s they find a United States embarking on a host of imaginative programs for the poor and unemployed and a Canada hell-bent on rugged individualism.

Despite these problems, Horowitz's analytical tour de force provides an invaluable legacy. It alerts us to the continuing power of ideas and influences not directly tied to the economy in explaining the enduring power of the Canadian left. It also reminds both leftists and historians that in any explanation of the Canadian left they need to pay attention to the peculiarities of Canada itself.[1]

That point brings us to another shortcoming of much of the existing writing on the Canadian left. Sometimes Canada disappears altogether: it is merely the empty stage upon which the timeless international play of class conflict and socialist struggle is eternally re-enacted, like anywhere else on the continent. Sometimes, though, exactly the opposite happens: Canada becomes such a huge presence that "its" interests are obviously the interests of all. Neither version approaches Canada as a political problem in and of itself.

For a historian wary of "essences," the word "Canada" is best viewed as a name for a process rather than a thing—in a way, more like a verb than a noun. Initially, "to Canada" northern North America meant making it correspond to the values and goals of the British liberalism that was a dominant world force precisely in the years (1840s–90s) when the new Canadian state in northern North America was acquiring its central, enduring institutions. The left has been profoundly influenced, on every level, by the power and durability of this multifaceted liberal project, whose power goes well beyond the formal political realm and which has been unusually successful in world terms. When we think of liberal order, the Liberal Party of Canada obviously comes to mind as one of the most successful parties in the Western world. The only successful political alternative on the federal level so far has been a Conservative Party—the *Liberal* Conservative and *Progressive* Conservative Party through much of the country's history.

Still, it would be a mistake simply to equate the *liberal order* for which those two parties stand and the *capitalist system* that they also undoubtedly defend. It is possible to have capitalist societies that are not governed by liberal orders (contemporary Malaysia, Singapore, or, arguably, China, for instance). It is also possible to find liberals in history who were not deeply involved in industrial capitalism (the aristocrats who were so often liberals in nineteenth-century Britain, Russia, and France, for example). Rather than an equation, we are dealing with a sort of "elective affinity," a subtler connection between the liberal order and the capitalist system. In Canada, under the auspices of liberalism, capitalism as a mode of production became ever more important. Much nineteenth-century liberalism called for the removal of those restrictions that impeded the growth of a capitalist economy. The protectionist National Policy in 1879, which the Liberal Conservatives brought in to nurture industries and integrate what had been separate export economies into a more cohesive domestic market, was a turning point in placing capitalist priorities at the centre of the liberal vision. Significantly, when the Liberals succeeded the Conservatives in power in 1896, they did not demolish, but rather improved, this tariff framework, even though they had spent the previous decade whipping up Canadians in denunciations of it.[2]

Many socialists writers and activists write as if "capitalism" directly shaped everything that happened in modern Canadian history. Capitalism oppresses the coal miners, their blood flows on the coal, the coal miners fight back—*et voilà*, the socialist tradition is born. Such simplifications overlook a basic reality. The everyday calamities of capitalism do not in themselves make for resistance. Only when the oppressed place those occurrences in an overall pattern—one different from that provided by conventional wisdom—do the events cause widespread political upheaval. From today's left point of view, writers can draw on the deaths of children in coal-mine disasters to demonstrate what was wrong about unregulated industrial capitalism in Canada, but for many people in the nineteenth century such tragedies might reveal the mysterious workings of Providence, the selfishness of parents who sent their children down the mine, or the wilfulness and carelessness of children who failed to do what they were told. As coal-mining families turned to socialism, they rejected these forms of explanation. They now saw the deaths of their children in the mine as the avoidable and damnable consequence of an unregulated capitalism. Fatalism and superstition were succeeded by anger and activism—as the "concrete utopia" of coal mines without grossly exploitive labour relations seized the working-class imagination.

In 1891, when the largest of Nova Scotia's mine disasters occurred, almost no one at the time connected the child-killing catastrophe with capitalism. In 1917 a disaster in the same province was explicitly linked to the irrationality and immorality of the entire system. The same thing goes with all the seemingly "objective facts" that the political economy of capitalism generates in such profusion. If today you are unemployed and homeless, you might say to yourself, "This is my own fault. I really should have worked harder." Or you might say, "I am part of a much larger social and economic process—every year a percentage of Canadians will be in my shoes, as part of the normal functioning of the economy. My individual problem is also a social problem." The system of concepts within which you place the objective fact makes all the difference as to what you think or do about it.

What is so striking about Canada is how deeply rooted and pervasive liberalism has been at all levels, as our default vocabulary for discussing the everyday calamities of capitalism. In fact, *Canada itself is a liberal project.* When you try to explain how such a state could come to exist on a continent so dominated by a republican superpower, and how it divided itself into two distinct and often mutually suspicious language groups, it pays to remember that what the mid-nineteenth-century founders of Canada, both French-speaking and English-speaking, wanted to achieve was precisely a liberal order counterpoised to the democratic experiment in the United States.

The relatively small elite group of liberal British North Americans—not many more, when all is said and done, than a few dozen white men—who were the exponents of the concept of Canadian Confederation were not a particularly original or far-sighted lot. But they were brilliant borrowers and synthesizers. They created an integrated framework of analysis that made possible, against steep odds, the formation of a liberal state project to rival that of the republican United States. Many students who go back to the major founding documents of the country, especially the British North America Act, are disappointed by the lacklustre language of a tedious text. Hoping to find great declarations of democratic principles and the rights of man and citizen, they find an endless succession of details. Who should administer the poor asylums? What about the lighthouses? Who gets Sable Island?

The document's one great memorable phrase is, tellingly, "Peace, Order, and good Government." The most powerful word in that triplet is "Order." No religious enthusiasms, no nationalisms, no Aboriginal revolts, no democratic debates, and no passions should enter into the heart of the Canadian political system.

Its main objective is a peaceful and good ordering. If people want to make their voices heard, let them do so *in order* and in an *orderly* way. (The unspoken corollary is that only some of them—on the basis of class, gender, and racial hierarchies—should be allowed to do so at all.)

If, as we are told so often, Canada was, even at its inception, a "liberal *democracy*," why were none of the founding documents of the dominion put before the democratic capacity to judge of the majority of the people? The answer, briefly, is that there was no such thing as a "Canadian people" in the founding documents of a dominion of order, and hence no citizens. There were only subjects of His or Her Majesty, normally resident in a British Dominion. Only those with certain property qualifications could be allowed into the Senate. There was no unanimity as to where political sovereignty resided—possibly with the Crown, or with the provincial governments, or the federal government, or some combination of the three—but only certifiable leftists believed that sovereignty, the final "buck stops here" of politics, should reside with the majority of the Canadian people.[3]

Even using Geoff Eley's narrow definition,* democracy is a new, tender shoot in Canadian soil. Through the 1930s and 1940s liberal governments used deportation, even if doing so raised the risk of the death of the deportees, as a method of political discipline. As late as 1940 many women were denied the vote at the provincial and federal levels simply because they were women. Canada's liberal rulers periodically denied the

---

* See p.25.

vote to racially defined groups of residents and, even through to the 1970s, to First Nations people on reserves. Down to the 1970s, against the resistance of the democratic left, both liberals and Liberals defended the War Measures Act, passed, among other draconian measures, as emergency legislation in the Great War and used to detain people without trial. (Even today self-respecting liberals seem capable of defending legislation that allows the state the right to detain suspects without even knowing the details of the case that has been brought against them, in brutal solitary confinement, *for years*).[4] Not only is the head of state a non-elected member of one particular family, but in a country made up of millions of people professing a diversity of religious faiths, and some no religious faith at all, this person must also by definition be the head of one particular Christian denomination; moreover, this position is defined in such a way that women are systematically discriminated against in favour of men. Yet the pervasive influence of liberal assumptions makes all of these flagrantly anti-democratic restrictions seem like the only way things can or should be done. One succinct definition of "the left" in Canada is that it consists of those who critique these restrictions. The left comprises those people who both advocate the full achievement of the legal terms of democracy and seek to ground formal democratic rights and freedoms in equitable and free social and economic relations.[5]

Once you agree with democracy as an ideal in either its strictly *formal* sense, or in this *broader* social sense, and open your eyes to its systemic violation in the letter and spirit of the liberal order around you, you then confront a difficult choice. You can act as a radical democrat and protest against these long-standing aspects of the society around you, with all the personal and political costs involved in such a choice; or you can silently withdraw into apathetic indifference and implicit consent. Democracy is, to echo Eley, not a "given" and it is not "granted." It emerges from forceful conflict, bold acts of defiance, and a willingness to court ridicule, marginalization, and victimization. In a Canada in which imprisonment without trial is defended by liberals, to be a democrat means breaking with a way of thinking and acting that has almost all the mass media and respectable political players on its side. It means abandoning the foundational code of "peace, order, and good government" for "the equal democratic empowerment of citizens." It means rethinking Canada at the most fundamental levels, in ways that are both liberating and painful. To be a liberal democrat is, in this context, to live in a state of denial about the force of qualification that the adjective "liberal" has historically exerted in Canada over that word "democrat." To be a consistent social democrat in a neo-liberal Canada with a relatively shallow and precarious commitment to civil liberties is, in this sense, an act that requires considerable courage.[6]

The liberals who founded Canada were possessed of political and social purpose, a driving sense of utopian possibility, and, best of all, a working model: that of Britain itself. They were, by virtue of the profound links of culture and politics that bound Canada to Britain, well-connected to the world's pre-eminent modern nation. The Canadian political and social history of the nineteenth century is in large measure the story of how the worldview of a few liberal men, living in a few southern cities, attained power over half a continent. They succeeded in writing a legal and historical text that became a political and social common sense over a huge expanse of the planet. They elaborated a liberal program that encompassed a diversity of peoples, many of whom they had never met and whose languages and cultures were entirely unfamiliar to them. They eventually claimed the second-largest land mass under the jurisdiction of any country in the world, much of which they had never seen. They managed to put together a constitutional formula and, more crucially, working political parties in which Catholics and Protestants and anglophones and francophones could park many of their fundamental differences at the door—provided they first agreed, implicitly or explicitly, with the vision of peace, order, and good government that the liberal order laid out for them. The architects of the Canadian state sharply disagreed with each other on how this vision should be realized. Should we, as John A. Macdonald's Liberal Conservatives urged after 1878, help industry by setting high tariffs in place? Or should we, as Wilfrid Laurier's Liberals urged down to the 1890s, help industry by establishing a continental union with the republican United States? Such debates were important. They were not fundamental. The "Right" (Tories) and the "Left" (Liberals) agreed with British definitions of freedom of speech and religion; with British parliamentary government; with the "civilization" and marginalization of the First Nations; and with the British model of the Industrial Revolution, under conditions of minimum interference with the freedom of entrepreneurs within their own "economic" sphere of activity. Down to

1900, they built a powerful political *order*—of laws in the Criminal Code, of schools, of government departments sworn to transform the "communist" customs of the First Nations—to make this utopian liberal projection a concrete reality. In this vision of liberal order, it was appropriate for the government to assist in the construction of railways, to protect Canadian industries, and to provide public education. It was largely beyond the pale to argue that the state should take over businesses, or even effectively to regulate them, let alone to conceive of the state as shaping the entire economy.

Liberal definitions of reality are part of our Canadian political and social tradition. The historian Fernande Roy speaks eloquently of a kind of "holy trinity" at the heart of liberal order: liberty, equality, and property.

- **Liberty:** for the *individual*, defined within liberalism not as a living human being but as the free-standing adult male who, within his private sphere, should be free to regulate his own activities without interference from the state.
- **Equality:** but only for such *individuals*, defined by their free-standing independence, who enjoy formal equality before the law (but not equality when it comes to their social conditions).
- **Property:** in many respects, the most fundamental principle of all, and the foundation of all the others: it is by holding property that the *individual* sustains his claim to recognition. (For the classical liberals of the mid-nineteenth century, even working for somebody else might damage your claim to be considered an individual and qualify your right to cast a ballot.)

On these grounds, the true liberals of the mid-nineteenth century might well argue against extending the right to vote to men without property or to the Aboriginal peoples they regarded as inferior because, in large measure, such people could never be true individuals. Some liberals, who scorned the very idea that females were "individuals" in the specific sense that they were using the term, delivered many of the most eloquent denunciations of the very idea of women's enfranchisement.[7]

Only slowly did this liberalism change. Only slowly, with pressure from the left, did the idea of democratic citizenship emerge tentatively and partially into this universe of liberal assumptions. Only slowly did the left achieve, against the massive and often violent resistance of corporate capital and the liberal state, a small measure of trade-union security and industrial democracy for working Canadians. The second great newspaper of the Canadian left was called *Citizen and Country*. The name was appropriate. To confront wavering and inconsistent liberals with a politico-ethical ideal of democratic citizenship has been the constant theme of Canadian left-wing history.

THE DANCE OF HEGEMONY

It may seem strange, but some of the most stimulating discussions for any understanding of the dynamics shaping this struggle for democracy can be found in the work of the Sardinian socialist Antonio Gramsci. A founder of the Communist Party of Italy and participant in the "red years" in Turin in 1919 and 1920, and a close student and critical supporter of the Russian

Revolution, Gramsci explored how a grassroots, revolutionary, democratic socialism might be organized in countries whose social and political landscape did not look much like the Russia that the Bolsheviks had transformed after 1917.

Gramsci argued that, as the members of powerful social groups came together, they first had to sort out their often rival economic ("corporate") interests and work out an understanding among themselves. Even if such men (far less commonly women) were rivals, they had to start to think in terms of the general interests and future of their group. Then, with their act more or less together, they had to take it on the road. They had to perform a politics that could draw in many other groups—even people with class interests completely opposed to themselves. This group had to secure its position of cultural and economic leadership through a combination of coercion and consent, in a never completely finalized, day-by-day process—one subject to mischief, misadventure, and miscalculation. They were also obliged to defend their project against rivals who threatened their grip on privilege and power, both economic and cultural. The show must go on, and on, and on: it is not grounded in eternal truths, but conscious human practices.

Gramsci calls this dance "hegemony." Hegemony too is a process, not a thing. It's a daily bid to achieve support for a political and social project, not a once-and-for-all achievement of total domination. Within the hegemonic group, you will always find rival interpretations of the general strategy. Outside the hegemonic group, you may well find people who want to challenge the very preconditions of the process. On the left, for example, the critics of liberal hegemony will keep pointing out that, for all the talk of "the nation" and "the people," some nations, races, genders, and classes are more equal than others.

Once a group, usually closely tied to a class, achieves hegemony, it works to make its historical choices—for instance, constructing a liberal order—seem to be just like natural phenomena, to which no sensible person can object. The language of the hegemonic group comes to seem like an ordinary, commonsense way of describing reality. You almost have to shake yourself to realize that, step by step, you have been drawn into a language game crafted for specific purposes that you actually have no real interest in serving. "Hegemony is a complex political and ideological process by which a society comes to appear a coherent whole built on consensus and unity," as one apt distillation puts it. "It means not only the domination of a particular political point of view, but also the tendency for other political views, and especially the recognition of conflicting interests (based, for example, on race, class, or gender), to be made invisible or, if visible, marginalized."[8]

The amazing pull of a right-wing politician such as George W. Bush provides an illustration of this dynamic. Why would average workers in Ohio vote for such a man, whose economic and social policies are very likely to undercut their own well-being? One old left-wing answer is that they are coerced into doing so, and that argument does take us a certain distance. The suspension of open trials and the abrogation of the rule of the presumption of innocence, the surreptitious recourse to torture, and the growth of the U.S. penitentiary population to gulag levels all remind democratic dissenters that stepping out of line can mean descending into hell. Another old answer emphasizes corruption, which again takes us a certain distance. The road to wealth is paved with untendered contracts for Iraqi reconstruction. But neither answer really captures why so many people, even in the privacy of the voting booth and with no government contract in their pockets, vote for someone whose apparent interests are diametrically and demonstrably opposed to their own.

Gramsci would begin to analyze this problem as a good example of what Canadians—with fresh memories of their own right-wing extremist regimes of the 1980s and 1990s—might ironically call a "Common Sense Revolution." Right-wing politicians of Bush's ilk succeed primarily because they create a political language that many people, workers included, strongly identify with. They often invoke dire warnings of immediate personal danger—the very disintegration of individuals if the politicians' words are not heeded and the wrong people are voted into office. They often speak powerfully to gendered ideals of manliness, heterosexuality, and hard work. Shouldn't individuals exert themselves? Shouldn't they strive to be God-fearing, decent, normal? Shouldn't they be free and independent? Shouldn't they have the right to their own hard-earned dollars, and not give them away to welfare recipients? Shouldn't we trim fat off the public service and fire bloated bureaucrats? Shouldn't we do away with a meddling state that's always telling individuals what to do? Shouldn't we respect people who through their own hard work have become successful and provide jobs for their fellow citizens? There is probably a little right-winger in everyone who has learned to think and speak politics in North America.

Instead of dismissing such implicit positions as symptoms of "false consciousness," a Gramscian tries to reconstruct how the system works hegemonically. This approach entails looking at the systems of ideas and values that make these extreme right-wingers seem to be speaking, to the majority of working people, words of reassurance and common sense. It means a close step-by-step analysis of the institutions that disseminate neo-liberal concepts. It means noticing that the daily language of politics is heavily imbued with many of these values and assumptions. They would be pervasive even if George W. Bush had failed to be re-elected in 2004. The problem is deeply lodged in the very language in which political questions are posed and answered, and in the performances that make this particular politics part of daily life—not just in the formal political sphere, but throughout civil society. To start thinking hegemonically is to start understanding the depth and subtlety of the problem posed to socialists by a successful ruling order, in ways that make earlier left analyses of the same problem—focused on coercion or corruption—seem superficial and simplistic.

This line of analysis does not come down to saying, idealistically, that if only we could change the ideological orientation of the majority, all would be well. Hegemony is not quite the same as "ideology." The theory of hegemony refers not just to ideological factors, but also to the material forms that generate these ideologies and to the social agents who may be attracted by them. Hegemony articulates not only ideas, but also, as Jonathan Joseph points out, "many practices—

ideological, cultural, political and economic, and the specific institutions of the state, civil society and the economy."[9] A "hegemonic project"—like that of the Canadian liberal order—not only functions at the level of ideas and images but also organizes people in economic and social life. This means that even to contest one of its core aspects—for example, the imprisonment and detention of political prisoners without trial—means questioning a vast network of assumptions, institutions, and values. What does it mean to build prisons? Why are torture and imprisonment without trial objectionable?

If you'd like to get a glimpse of Gramsci's insight, simply devote a day to keeping track of all the messages you receive from various media—newspaper editorials, television advertisements, radio talk shows, subway signs, highway billboards—about the virtues and benefits of our economic and political system. This is a far subtler business than routine left critiques of "propaganda" would lead us to believe. For example, take the seemingly neutral "business report" on CBC Newsworld and attend carefully to the language and metaphors packed into an average ten-minute slice of its "factual reporting." The TSX had a good day today: advances led declines. By whose definition does such a record mean a "good day"? Note the implicit choices made to give you one slice of reality over another. Notice which people and institutions—corporations, company presidents, investors—count as legitimate speakers and actors in this imaginary business worldview; and notice the missing people, the vast majority of human beings who, as mere producers of commodities and reproducers of human beings, are left out of this imagined universe altogether.

In this universe there is no such thing, nor should there be, as *society*—there are just investors, shareholders, consumers, individuals one and all, but all united in the common objective of making money. Notice how the entire system of signs celebrates and envelopes itself. What would it mean to break into this charmed circle to insert a radically different agenda? Look also at the form of the business news—streams of numbers generated from Tokyo, New York, London, Frankfurt that provide us with a mind-boggling flow of information. Like individuals gazing at the twinkling infinity of the night sky, we are meant to experience this sublime onrush of numerical data with a kind of pleasure and awe. These numbers, these multitudinous mythical places, these data streaming from every corner of the planet: how can we, mere mortals that we are, possibly even have a worthwhile opinion about any of this?

Day in and day out, the conviction builds: this is just the way things are. This is the way things have to be. There are no citizens in this imagined neo-liberal global world of the business report. There is only a multitude of companies, trust funds, corporations, portfolios, and businessmen—individuals one and all, performing the world economy every day on the national news. Our democratic right to object to this vast panorama of science and authority seems comically out of proportion with its constant projection of a magnificent spectacle. Without having ever to argue explicitly on behalf of a system that, on another level of analysis, is profoundly crazy and leading us to the brink of an environmental catastrophe, the report on business succeeds brilliantly in making British Prime Minister Margaret Thatcher's two pivotal philosophical and political arguments: (1) There Is No Such Thing As Society, and (2) There Is No Alternative. You can read the high-brow version of this worldview in *The Economist*, but the more accessible edition is available whenever you turn on your television set.[10]

Hegemony works at many levels to create a deep sense of the wholeness and rightness of the existing social and economic world and one's place, however humble, within it. For example, much of Canadian history—as presented, for instance, in the Heritage Minutes, People's History, and the "Ten Greatest Canadians" contest—implicitly persuades us of the inevitability and goodness of "Canada." Noticing the implicit agenda and challenging it can almost seem boorish. It means you "don't fit in." What you don't fit into is the daily, humdrum, average business of the normal world. Indeed, to be an influential public intellectual today—a television host, a newspaper editorial writer, or an economic pundit—requires believing that no other world is possible (and, in a subtler sense, that no other social world than this one has ever really existed). As they say in cyberspace, what you see is what you get—and that's all you're ever going to get. It means living in the here and now, not in the future or in the past (or in a world in which both past and future are co-present).

Nearly every television commercial is a mini-sermon on the impossibility of living otherwise: there can only ever be an eternal process of adaptation to the demands of a market. The overall purpose of these market transactions is far beyond the comprehension of any individual, or any group of human beings. But notice that the television commercials are not just about "ideas." They are themselves also commodities, helping to organize consumers and producers in economic life. There is a deep structural hegemony at work here—one that goes to the reproduction of basic social structures and practices—as well a conscious hegemony—the expression of social values and worldviews. They are two sides of the same process.

Liberal hegemony works at the deepest levels—organizing our jobs and our economic existence—as well as on the more visible and contestable levels of formal politics. Once you start to trace particular problems to the economic and political forces that generate them, and once you start to think about the general preconditions of any living otherwise, it is hard to avoid concluding that the entire economic and social structure, including the state, must be completely transformed. Given that articulate and far-sighted liberals began to craft that state in the 1840s, shaping a constitution profoundly influenced by their assumptions; given that they can draw on the "common sense" of a capitalist system that seems to ratify their reverence for the free-standing individual; and given that they have vast cultural and symbolic resources, entire disciplines of knowledge, even theological systems, that are complementary to their construction of reality—given all this and more, the battle would seem to be over before it has begun.

Yet, it is not over. Capitalism is not a stable system. It generates crisis after crisis, some obviously rooted in its basic economic processes and others in its opaque and subtle socio-cultural circuitry. In each crisis opportunities arise for the left. The contingents of the left would vanish tomorrow were it not for the awkward fact that they can articulate truths that will always evade even the most aggressive articulation of liberal hegemony. The liberal order, which provides the terms in which capitalist social and economic realities are understood, is shot through with contradictions that can hardly find expression, let alone solution, in its own terms. One major advantage of the Canadian left—when compared at any rate with that of its contemporary U.S. counterpart—has been that these contradictions have never been far from the surface. They cannot be papered over with a domineering nationalism that rules left questions out of court before they can even be posed.

In Canada liberal order was imposed externally on societies and traditions with quite different histories (the First Nations and Quebec, for example). It then confronted sustained and serious internal challenges. It regularly confronts evidence that, in a fundamental sense, there is a human need to belong and to knit together in communities and societies. Churches and community choirs, charities and sports events, service clubs and folk festivals all suggest this enduring need for community—a need that acquisitive individualism cannot satisfy. Yet this search for community takes place in a context of intensifying atomization. There remains a widely dispersed sense of "quiet desperation" in this society. Mass depression and suicide haunt the contemporary modern world. Free-market societies report ever-declining rates of personal happiness. By and large, as impressively documented empirical studies confirm, advanced consumerist materialism erodes, rather than satisfies, a sense of well-being.

As deep, non-commercial ties between people become ever weaker, loneliness in life and solitude at death are the predictable fates of a growing number of people. In this cold liberal order, millions of lonely individuals turn to antidepressants (a major postwar growth industry) or medicate themselves with alcohol and other drugs because their lives have become desperate struggles against sadness. They are tiny, replaceable parts in an unpredictable machine no one can remember making. Their desolation reflects a much broader lack of any real autonomy or purpose throughout contemporary society. Often, even when they think they're outside the machine—when they go on prepackaged tours, for instance—they've just entered another one of its parts. "There Is No Alternative," the neo-liberal slogan of the epoch, is not merely a Thatcherite mantra but an everyday experience. Few of the people who repeat it seem to notice that it chillingly echoes the certainty of every recent totalitarianism.[11]

The hegemonic system can sell you Prozac or a vacation. It can engulf you in a fear of "Terror." It cannot close over the real sense of disconnection between the wholeness and happiness it promises and the reality it delivers. People go through the motions at work to acquire money and consume more things. By consuming more things, they find they have to put in more hours of work. Links between people become ever more tenuous and calculating in an ever-colder neo-liberal world. Its inhabitants confront a vast universe, in the shopping malls but also in their own living rooms, made up of objects external to themselves, over which they have little control—what Marx, following and adapting the teachings of the philosopher Hegel—would call the experience of "alienation." We treat the natural world with thoughtless indifference. We treat other people as so many "human resources." We treat ourselves with drugs, alcohol, or escapism. We treat our political leaders with ill-disguised contempt. We treat the language we share with others as though it were a thing that can be "spun" and "spun again" to achieve selfish objectives. We rarely give ourselves even a moment to gather ourselves together and reflect on the destruction that all this frantic rushing and grabbing entail for the people and things around us.

At night neighbourhoods glow with the blue light of television as one by one, alone in our living rooms, we seek to repair the damage that the loss of community has caused. History itself becomes a mass phenomenon of organized forgetfulness. Biographies, cop shows, Musique-Plus, a televangelist marketing heaven for the believers and hell for everybody else—and so, bleary-eyed, to bed. The humanity we cannot find in our jobs and our neighbourhoods can be located, if only for a short time and in a partial, unsatisfying way, in chat-rooms and web-sites, a diversity of "temporary autonomous zones," islands of freedom in a universe of necessity.

Little personal acts of resistance, efforts to connect with someone in the vast silence of post-social space, isolated attempts to grasp and to theorize its patterns, simply shutting off the television or reaching out for "community"—these are the inaugural gestures of resistance. They are not to be minimized. Yet, if they stay there—in the temporary autonomous zones, in the isolated experiences, in the purely theoretical breakthroughs in the university seminar room or the critical academic journal—they quickly fade away. The "freedom" that such experiences create is confined to one person or one family, one moment of intoxication, one classroom. They do not generate a counter-world. Insofar as they heighten an individualistic sense of superiority and refinement, they may even be swiftly transformed into experiences as alienating as the ones they protest. Often, in the sites in which we try to imagine freedom—"heritage," wilderness, adventure, even evangelical religion—we are reintroduced, once the opiate fades, to the ambient exhaust fumes of dread and ennui in a social and cultural system that we had hoped to escape forever. The "problem that has no name" has not gone away, and the pretended solutions—the marketing of heritage, the construction of wilderness, the selling of personal adventure, the wonders of televangelism—are just further demonstrations of it. As Zygmunt Bauman observes in *In Search of Politics*, "Ideology used to set reason *against nature*; the neo-liberal discourse disempowers reason through *naturalizing* it."[12] The new liberalism—really the old classical liberalism with a fiercer sense of its own totalitarian grasp of reality and a much wider theatre of operation—sets out systematically and "rationally" to remove even the memory of alternatives to itself.

The contemporary left critique of capitalism and the liberal order certainly focuses on their material implications: the environmental devastation, the widening gap between the tiny numbers of the very rich and the swelling numbers of the impoverished and homeless. But it also extends to the sheer crass banality of capitalism, the insipid and cruel world of television spectacle, the way in which we treat each other and ourselves as so many inanimate objects.[13]

The Gramscian point is not that defiance of this vast alienating world is futile. It is that resistance is both necessary and difficult. To make any lasting difference, resistance can be neither merely individual nor narrowly class-defined. To become genuinely effective, acts of opposition must engage with the underlying economic and social processes that structure the entire system. If, like much middle-class cultural work today, acts of resistance come from a space of alienated and angry fatalism, they simply ratify the impression that there is nothing worthwhile or permanent to be done. They add their little bit to an ambient sense of futility. If you want a genuinely democratic realm of freedom, where you might enjoy more than a momentary respite from the iron machinery of capital, you have to understand the subtle ways in which the system shapes its subjects, and you have to achieve this compassionate understanding in the company of other people. This is not a minor undertaking. It is a life's commitment.

In speaking of how to create resistance, Gramsci contrasted a "war of manoeuvre" with a "war of position." The war of manoeuvre might be thought of in terms of the classic Russian Revolution script for an upheaval that overpowers the state. Build a disciplined body of seasoned revolutionaries, seize the Winter Palace, and let the New Day begin. Some people have discerned the potential for such a revolutionary moment at various times and places in Canadian history—Winnipeg 1918–19 or Montreal 1965–70 (to cite just two examples).

Such moments might well come again. Imagine that five years from now, after tremendous economic and social chaos, a revolutionary party seizes power in Ottawa. The very next day they—we—would have to ask ourselves: "How are we going to manage the Bank of Canada? Should there be advertising on TV? Should there be TV at all? How should we supply power to our cities? How would a new society build cars—if it does build cars? How are we going to hand over power to the people so that they don't need revolutionary leaders like us any more, but can make up their own minds? And now that we're here, where are the people who can generate the information we need to do any of this?" Seizing Parliament Hill and Rideau Hall begins to look less and less like a defining moment. Like it or not, unless we as revolutionaries simply wanted to be new bosses acting very much like the old bosses, we would be confronted with all the questions of hegemony and popular power that Gramsci tried to analyze as he wrote in his fascist prison cell. Either the democratic revolution had already been well launched—or the seizure of power would amount to a mere coup d'état, not a genuine social and cultural transformation.[14]

THE WAR OF POSITION

In most Western countries, a far likelier prospect for the left than a "war of manoeuvre" is that of a prolonged "war of position," a kind of "reciprocal siege" (citing Gramsci once again) in which rival political projects compete over a long period. Ultimately our way of life needs to be changed from top to bottom—or we are not truly living otherwise. But in order for that change to mean something more than a cosmetic renaming of the elite that rules us, there would have to be an enormous struggle beforehand and afterwards to change the very common sense of politics. The war of position means that the party of democracy engages, over decades, in a struggle to change minds and challenge policies. It struggles to disseminate its different view of the social order. Often it plays the language of liberalism against itself. It struggles on a hundred fronts. It develops a different way of seeing the world. It fights for the revolution, but in slow motion.

As the Canadian case so clearly demonstrates, the risk of the "war of position" is that, over time, the project of the left can become unfocused and compromised. The Liberal Party in Canada is the past master of the arts of co-optation and selective absorption. As soon as it perceives a profound crisis in the system it is capable of making concessions, even ones that are unpopular with business. It proclaims, day in and day out, its fierce loyalty to the democratic values that it has historically resisted. It works to "decapitate" the radical movements of their leaders and, over time, to incorporate into its own activities those of their demands that do not place the entire liberal order and capitalist system in question. It offers a compromise through which substantial concessions to popular demands are made—but with the price tag that grassroots democratic movements edit out their radical leaders, soften up their politics, and learn how to play the liberal game. Such is the logic of "passive revolution." It involves a dynamic of both revolution (because far-reaching concessions are made) and restoration (because the intended outcome is to remove the teeth from the liberal order's most consistent critics). How to prevent a "war of position" from falling into a liberal "passive revolution" is a question that has vexed every major left formation in Canada.

Every major leftism in Canadian history has ultimately been digested by the liberal order. Such can be the stuff of ironic or tragic narrative. It is also possible to view this record more radically and, in a sense, pragmatically. Each "utopian projection" from the left has transformed the world—never nearly as much as its militants had hoped, but often far more than the liberal order had been initially prepared to concede. The partial achievement of democracy and civil liberties we enjoy today would not have happened without, and is now only really understood and defended by, the activists of the left.

The entire social welfare state, public medicine most obviously, is always under threat from the forces of the right, who rightly perceive in it a subtle and pervasive challenge to the individualism they champion. From the hegemonic perspective of liberalism, the most suspect element of public medicine is that it decommodifies aspects of social life that could potentially be enormously lucrative for investors, all in the name of a concept of the "social" that neo-liberalism hoped to have buried long ago. But, although always endangered by the ruling regime, such concessions to democracy cannot easily be abolished by it.

A left that has never held power in Canada as a whole has nonetheless mounted a powerful struggle. Thanks to the left, the definition of "Canada" must now include, at least in some aspects of life, the notion of the "social democratization" of northern North

America. It is not the utopian project that the left demanded, but in the context of a continent consumed by an increasingly "totalizing" politics of fear and right-wing extremism, it is also not chopped liver. It suggests that writing the history of the left as one "failure" after another only superficially engages with its contradictory impact upon historical events. That we even have a left whose future can be debated is an achievement.

The system under which we live generates fundamental and deep-seated—Gramsci would say "organic"—crises, which manifest themselves in countless events and moments in daily life. In Canada, since the 1840s, the ruling regime, and the system of concepts that it works with to make a "common sense," contain the implications of these events by categorizing them in familiar ways. Even in the face of contradictions that seem unfathomable, conventional opinion reaches for the tried-and-true nostrums, maxims, and slogans. A good example is capitalism's great interwar economic depression (dramatized but not begun by the stock-market crash of 1929). The collapse of regional economies, the bankruptcy of municipalities and provincial governments, the ecological catastrophe of the dust bowl on the Prairies—all could be "understood," in a way, through a liberal political-economic theory tracing such events to the actions of individuals. When it came to policy-making, the same individualistic conceptual framework could apply. The unemployed were individually responsible for their position. However grave the economic catastrophe, it did not suggest that, in many fundamental respects, the capitalist system itself had malfunctioned. It was just a business downturn. It was only through the rise of a new state-building left in the 1930s, with an alternative language of politics and conception of the social order, that such complacent notions could be shaken. Yet there was, and is, a limit beyond which a liberal order cannot go. Far-reaching changes—family allowances, unemployment insurance, trade union security—should hardly be dismissed as merely cosmetic. They made a substantial difference to the functioning of the system and its impact on ordinary human beings. Yet they left intact, and arguably strengthened, the capitalist system whose crisis they were intended to address. Having made these changes within the liberal order, the Liberal Party could embark on the construction of a postwar order in which the left challenge would be forcibly marginalized.

The contemporary environmental crisis will present a similar fundamental challenge to the hegemonic order. Initially, as with the Great Depression of the 1930s, the hegemonic response has been to conceptualize the problem in the individualistic terms central to liberal order. Individuals are urged to recycle their newspapers and pop bottles. Cities ban smoking in public spaces. The problem is that the environmental crisis, like the Depression, cannot be addressed in the language of individualism. Reasoning the environment crisis otherwise, living it otherwise, means beginning with radically different premises than those available to liberalism. It means questioning the capitalist system itself. But how does one construct such alternative conceptualizations in ways that make them more powerful than mere polemical gestures or academic mind games?

Alternative left systems of concepts that move thousands of people to think and act otherwise do not emerge spontaneously from the soil of popular struggles, but they must also somehow connect with those struggles. Left-wing formations invariably have a limited socio-economic range and only so much time—on the Canadian average, about a quarter-century—to act as the nucleus of the wider left, itself lodged within a liberal order that it does not control. What is key to any evaluation of their success or failure is an assessment of the long-term structural changes that can plausibly be traced back to their influence. During the life span of a particular left project as it appeared in the crevices of liberal order, how much change did it effect? How hard was this one to assimilate—and what were the (foreseen and unforeseen) consequences of its incorporation?

Thinking in this way places in a different light the whole question of "reform vs. revolution" that exercised much of the Canadian left through the twentieth century. It is quite possible, for instance, to regard oneself as a complete revolutionary, identifying with a "homeland of the revolution," reading revolutionary theorists all day long and belonging to a revolutionary party and not, ultimately, manage to say or build anything with lasting revolutionary—that is, system-challenging—significance. Conversely, it is equally possible to regard oneself as a mild-mannered, middle-of-the-road, pragmatic reformist, without any interest in blood and thunder—and to say words and do things that lead people to act in system-challenging ways. In all of this, much depends on how subtly the arts of hegemony are learned and how skilfully applied—and on the times in which one is living.

FOUR

The Strategy of Reconnaissance

ONE DAY IN 2001 I was reading an old book about Edward Bellamy, one of North America's most popular prophets of socialism in the nineteenth century. The point of the book was to show that Bellamy, however much he inspired people in his own time, should be seen as an ominous portent of the authoritarian socialism of the twentieth century. On one of its pages I came across a note, apparently scribbled by the book's previous owner: "To write like this, seeing all politics as either essentially rt. [right] or wrong, is a 'scorecard' approach. There are no full steam attempts to understand why the wrong are as they are—same for the rt."[1]

Exactly. This "scorecard approach" is pervasive today. Understandable and useful in one way, it reflects an unthinking, deep liberalism in another. It assumes that individuals should be held strictly accountable for conceptual frameworks that operate far beyond the control of any one of them. Sectarian exercises in scorecard history will confirm the values of the present-day leftist, over and over and over again. If we already know what the score is going to be, why go to the trouble of watching the game? Apart from this futility, what bothers me most about scorecard history is the hubristic arrogance of believing that any historian can infallibly bestow or deduct points.

As an alternative to scorecard history I suggest a strategy of "reconnaissance." The word literally means "a preliminary examination or survey, as of the territory and resources of a country." It carries a second military meaning of "the act of obtaining information of military value, especially regarding the position, strength, and movement of enemy forces." Both meanings suit my purpose. A left historian is engaged in obtaining information of use in the lengthy war of position that, as Gramsci observed, Western leftists necessarily fight. What exists in Canada, in terms of underlying economic and political structures, is capitalism and liberal order. In addition to knowing the ruling regime's strengths and weaknesses, we also need to pass on what has been learned by past generations about how to survive and thrive in such a setting. How does it work? Where are the major landforms? The bivouacs? The land mines? Where is this regime vulnerable? How can we use our own twenty-five years or so to best occupy this terrain?

A reconnaissance is several steps down the ladder of comprehensiveness from a polished and final synthesis. Reconnaissance is a way of summing up a different way of thinking about the history of the left. When leftists write the history of their movements, they often fall into the trap of reading back into past political realities all the terms and conditions of the present. Hoping to write politically useful histories, they often simply echo present-day polemics. In a way, such traditional left historians are conservatively trying to reassure present-day leftists that their conceptual systems rest upon permanent rock-solid foundations. One point of reconnaissance, both in real life and in metaphor, is to awaken us to little-explored realities, in an age when, philosophically and politically, the quest for such rock-solid foundations seems more and more quixotic.

At the same time a reconnaissance entails something other than the pursuit of knowledge for its own sake, for the amusement and edification of the reader. Reconnaissance is a political act of research. Reconnaissance is not a strategy that says, in effect, "it does not matter if one side or the other dominates a question or the pace and direction of change." Actually, as the rise of the extreme right in the United States reveals, these questions of interpretation matter a great deal. A second point of reconnaissance is to produce knowledge for a political purpose—in this case, to help a re-emergent Canadian left see its history more clearly and define its present more strategically.

WORKING WITH A LEGACY

In the twenty-first century the very word "socialism" has become an epithet. Often a complicated history that unfolded over a century and a half is depicted in harsh and misleading slogans. The socialist bequest to modern activists contains so many divisive and controversial clauses that contemporary activists can be forgiven for wanting to wipe the slate clean and start again—with grassroots anarchism, international social justice movements, massive anti-state mobilizations. As each new cycle of leftism begins—and one is plainly beginning now—generationally minded activists may well feel the need to mark their distance with an older cohort: "That was then, and this is now."

Yet from the late nineteenth century to the present the major systemic challenges to liberal order in Canada have identified themselves with the achievements of socialism. Now, as the new century evolves, leftists will very likely find a different name for their project—but they are nonetheless the inheritors of the past movements, even if they see that legacy as a mixed blessing. Leftists who cut themselves off from the radical past end up paying a high price: for one thing we deny ourselves access to important sources of information and inspiration. If left-wing effectiveness in Canada comes down in large part to how skilfully and subtly liberal order is pushed to its definitional limits, and then some, those embarked on the new left project have everything to gain from a critical understanding of the prior efforts of past leftists, without any implication that they necessarily share all of the same political means and ends. Thinking back through the past Canadian generations of those who wanted to live otherwise can provide a sense of perspective when a new generation, or even later generations, come to weigh their tactics and strategies.

Radical historicism means regarding the present moment as a "historical problem." In so doing, it directly challenges the doctrine of "There Is No Alternative" by illustrating the almost infinitely wide range of socio-cultural arrangements that human beings have put to work throughout history. For example, one of the great inspirations for socialist feminism as it developed from the 1880s to the 1970s was the anthropological evidence that, historically, other societies had functioned with very different patterns of gender relations. This knowledge provided a powerful argument against those who regarded women's subordinate position simply as the recognition of natural necessity. If you apply radical historicism to the history of radicalism itself, that means you are looking at yourself as the carrier of a generations-old tradition of reasoning and living otherwise, neither exalting your own individual importance nor minimizing the extent to which your words and actions might possibly make a difference to others. To lose any sense of making history in this sense robs present-day activism of theoretical and ethical ballast. It leaves radicals without important ways of distancing themselves from a hegemonic apparatus that is only too willing to convert their lives and words into marketable commodities.

Without a historically defined "affinity group," leftists are tempted to define success or failure in the terms of the society surrounding them. In *A Long Way from Home*, an eloquent, underrated study of the radical 1960s in English Canada, Myrna Kostash points out this problem in connection with the militants in the Student Union for Peace Action (SUPA), by some measures English Canada's leading New Left group. These activists, she writes, tended to draw their analysis in "very broad strokes, as though SUPA inhabited a metasociety in which the categories of action, violence, class and power applied not to any particular social place but to all places."[2] Their analyses, in short, lacked the historical specificity and depth that would allow them to meaningfully regard their own society and their own times as historical problems. Radical ahistoricism underwrites the acquisitive individualism rampant through liberal order, because it rules out any possibility that we, as present-day activists, are connected with older forms of activism.

This tendency also, paradoxically, feeds more directly than does sober historical analysis into a kind of fatalistic acquiescence to the inevitability of liberal order. Liberals have been writing obituaries for the left in Canada since at least 1911 (indeed, the first major book-length study of socialism in Canada was a critique purporting to show that it would be a complete non-starter in the Dominion). Ever since then liberals have been confronted with remarkable left-wing resurrections. It is true that the left has never been hegemonic in Canada. The "party of socialists" (to use Marx's all-inclusive phrase) has never had the power to set the general terms or language of political debate. Yet, at least when they are on their game and have a favourable opportunity, leftists too have engaged in effective hegemonic politics. (For clarity's sake we might call this left strategy one of "counter-hegemony," even though Gramsci himself did not favour this expression.) A genuine "party of the left" has to struggle to make its own reading of reality pervasive and influential, no matter what the odds. Otherwise it is just treading water. Just like those it opposes, it too must articulate ways of getting beyond immediate interests and move towards a more general strategy in which those interests are expressed. It too must speak of a people or a nation. It too must think beyond the present moment to encompass a long-term notion of change through time. It has to learn how to speak a "common sense" that the majority of people can identify with.[3]

Curiously enough, in the seemingly inhospitable Canadian climate, many important left assumptions have become part of the political and cultural common sense. If removed from its polemical or political context and regarded more coolly and analytically, the pervasive and overwhelming support for a health-care system that palpably incarnates left principles of universality and equality is a striking indication of the ability of the Canadian left to intervene, at some times and in some places, in ways that have plainly made a major difference to millions of people. So too is Canada's unusually elevated level (in continental terms) of trade-union organization (although labour economists do warn that private-sector unionism is declining rapidly). The highly visible profile and initial successes of First Nations struggles and the identification of Canadian foreign policy with peacekeeping are other examples. They all suggest the paradoxical ability of the left, unable to challenge liberal order frontally and centrally, to use the country's very heterogeneity to further a democratic agenda. In a country that resembles an archipelago of distinct communities more than a unitary nation, democratic breakthroughs have tended to be local. For that very reason, by fortifying themselves with local traditions and providing concrete benefits, leftists have tended to withstand pressures from the centre. The much-lamented absence of one big "integral" nationalism in Canada has been an enormous boon to the left, because in its absence the hegemonic order is deprived of the tool of xenophobic patriotism that elsewhere—especially in the United States—has been, alongside evangelical Protestantism, the most efficacious anti-democratic weapon of them all. In Canada, to mount a crusade against the legacy of Tommy Douglas and the achievement of a public health system because they are "un-Canadian" would be a difficult rhetorical stretch, even for the likes of right-wing newspapers such as the *National Post*, *Ottawa Citizen*, or *The Globe and Mail*.

In large measure policies that draw on the socialist tradition have survived in regional pocket-editions because they have been shown to work fairly well for most people. Canadian decentralized federalism, implicitly designed to accommodate liberalism and frustrate democracy, has unintentionally also made room for a plethora of post-liberal democratic experiments. None of them, I hasten to add, measure up fully to the challenge of living otherwise—like Canada itself, they bear all the marks of patchwork and paste. Yet taken singly and together, they do make this a different terrain for the left than that seen in the United States, a country that otherwise Canada very much resembles. Moreover, unlike Australia, New Zealand, the Netherlands, France, and Britain—other countries that have "lefts" that can be profitably compared with our own—Canadian socialists have never been called upon to govern in the country as a whole. Socialists have been strong enough to influence, sometimes even, in times of Liberal minority governments, to write, the laws; they have never been absorbed by the state bureaucracy that enforces them.

What makes the bequest from the past awkward in the eyes of present-day activists is not just the misleading impression of historical insignificance, but the more damaging question of moral ambiguity. The word "socialism" has barely survived the twentieth century because of its adoption by a succession of murderous regimes, on the right as well as on the left. After entering the twentieth century as a vague but radiant promise, "socialism" exited it carrying the odium of promises betrayed. As Eley remarks:

> Stalinism's ferocities during the 1930s and 1940s did irremediable damage to Communism's ethical credibility . . . enabling associative allegations against all other versions of socialist ideas. Justified reminders of capitalism's destructive and genocidal consequences for the world, both inside Europe and without, can never dispose of those histories, as fuller knowledge of Bolshevism's post-1917 record is making ever more clear.[4]

And yet, as Eley goes on to remark, the European left has more often rejected than accepted violent strategies.

The Canadian setting has spared socialists some of these difficulties. Most of Canada's most obvious human rights disasters—policies of Aboriginal assimilation, the shameful record of prejudice against Jewish immigrants in the 1930s, the deportation of political dissidents, the Cold War persecutions of homosexuals and critical thinkers, and today the imprisonment without trial of suspects—cannot be attributed to leftists. The burden of responsibility for the most glaring offences against "liberal democracy" must be borne by liberals themselves. Then too, the very impossibility of producing one authoritative "socialist voice" in Canada has, paradoxically, made space for many different ways of talking and acting on the left. In practice, the Canadian left has tended to work on a principle of "subsidiarity"—that is, that decisions should be made at the level closest to those most directly affected by them. Perhaps because of this, and to a surprising extent, the Canadian left has withstood the vast international backlash that has levelled the left through much of the rest of the world, including Britain, France, and the United States, countries that Canadian leftists have often regarded as more advanced models for their own movement.

In an understated way, the Canadian left has perhaps achieved a balance that has eluded leftists in other places. One of its strengths is that it has always been a plural left. All the "lefts" are united by a shared language of socialism, but each speaks a different dialect and raises particular problems and issues. There certainly have been some Canadian leftists who have apologized for contemptible regimes. Yet the suffocating, ideologically blinkered, tyrannous tendencies to which these right-wingers have devoted so many books, and which they have dramatized so effectively in their denunciations of the "God That Failed," are not imposing specimens in the pragmatic Canadian context. When *The Toronto Star* endorsed Communist candidates for city hall in the late 1930s, or postwar Winnipeggers elected Joe Zuken as their Communist alderman year after year, they were not caught up in some delusional notion that such leftists spoke for a secular "God." They were just supporting or electing left-wing politicians who they thought would be honest and competent civic officials. The same might be said of the many trade unionists, warned of the terrible consequences they were risking, who phlegmatically elected far-leftists to office year after year in the 1980s and 1990s, convinced on good evidence that Communists of various descriptions often made very able trade unionists.[5]

Long before it became an international fashion trend, the Canadian left was a movement of movements. Even within the Communist Party, which made a determined effort to stamp out federalism in its struggles to live up to the Bolshevik model in the 1920s, the centralism much touted in Leninist theory was always a tough sell in poly-ethnic and poly-regional practice. What looked great to some people in Toronto—a monolithic party obeying revolutionary orders—did not quite look the same when translated into Finnish in Northern Ontario. The variety of ways of talking and acting on the left have been well adapted to their particular constituencies. Some of these have been remarkably successful, in their time and place. Thus one of the things that is wrong with the dominant liberal historiography on Canadian socialism, with its ironic tone and easy dismissals, is the unitary conception that it has formed of its left-wing adversary. It actually makes more sense, and aligns better with the evidence, to speak of "Canadian socialisms." If all of the variations shared a common language of socialism, each had its own distinctive dialect and nurtured its own sense of its history.

Yet once we disable this liberal narrative line on the socialist tradition—a line holding that socialism is both easily encompassed in a simple formula and now, thankfully, consigned to the past—what do we set in its place? Surely not another combination of sectarianism and sentimentality?

BEYOND SCORECARDS: MATRIX-EVENTS

Objectivity, historian Thomas Haskell usefully remarks, is not neutrality.[6] The pragmatically useful knowledge of the past produced by repeated exercises in reconnaissance won't be particularly useful for people who have no interest in living otherwise. A useful reconnaissance of Canadian socialism involves no ancestor worship of past socialists, and no sense of certainty that ultimately the "right side" is going to win. It may actually involve sightings of once-promising paths that turned out to be dead ends. Neither trial by jury nor exculpation by biography, reconnaissance nonetheless explores such paths because doing so can suggest important parallels with contemporary strategic alternatives. If, for example, you dream today of creating a Leninist vanguard party in Canada, along the lines of the party that made the Bolshevik Revolution, you have everything to gain from a sober consideration of the three dozen or so earlier attempts to create similar vanguard organizations. What worked? What failed? How long did such experiments normally last? How did people who went through them evaluate the experience afterwards? What lasting, system-changing impact did they have? To be useful, reconnaissance has to make such inquiries, in terms that are as open to empirical verification and disconfirmation as possible. Ideally, the results of a reconnaissance should be put in such a way that they can be overthrown by contrary evidence—and not just by appeals to scriptural authority.

Like the founders of liberal order in the 1840s, the aspiring founders of a left democratic order, few in number, uncertain, and divided on many profound grounds, must nonetheless devise a means of grasping this terrain of their history. And, as Gramsci said, exploring these possibilities of genuine freedom—the possibilities for political and social change that we find in such profusion in the past—is not yet enough; it is necessary to "know" them, to integrate them into our understanding of the present, to see our own present day as a "historical problem." In other words, if we want to *live otherwise*, we have to live our present differently. We have to re-experience the past as a way of re-anticipating our future. We have to imagine generations of radicals past and generations yet to come as our co-investigators and co-activists—not as people standing before us at the bar of history, awaiting our God-like judgment. In our present politics we have to go beyond our immediate interests to create ways of linking up with people who can become political allies, without sacrificing Marx's core insights into the fundamental contradictions of the system. *We have to begin to think hegemonically*. This point also applies to how we construct the past and the future. We have to transcend our immediate temporal limitations to re-create the ways of thinking and seeing that many previous radical democrats identified with, so that we can more clearly understand their leftisms. We have to have an acute and respectful awareness of the political and social order that we want to change—and an equally precise sense of the many attempts made before us to change it.

Undertaking a reconnaissance means probing each left formation for its rational core, its answer to the recurrent problems that liberal order generates for anyone who wants to live otherwise. It is also a strategy that reflects (to a point) developments in social and cultural theory over the past years. Instead of assuming that individuals, or groups of individuals, attain "identities" that are fixed and stable over long periods of time, it assumes that identity-formation is always a much more fluid, ambiguous, and contradictory process. Instead of assuming that we can plot historical events on a straight line stretching back to the earliest days and forward to the known future, it assumes that every event can be placed within many perspectives. Instead of assuming that ideological and cultural formations such as socialism merely passively reflect underlying social structures, it assumes that they dynamically interact and, on occasion, even transform those structures. Instead of seeing the subjects of history as so many experimental objects, it sees them as our contemporaries and equals, engaged in decades-long conversations about how to live otherwise. It refuses, in other words, the comforting idea that we radicals of today are much more sophisticated and intelligent than the people about whom we write.

A radical-democratic reconnaissance contrasts with a mainstream academic synthesis. My image of the latter is that of a white-coated scientist in a laboratory, his individual genius demonstrated by a blackboard covered with equations. He is coolly holding a beaker—containing the "synthesis"—in his hand. My image of reconnaissance is that of an advance scout returning to the home base. The scout holds a report, spotted with drops of sweat, prepared under pressure, on the heterogeneity and surprises of a little-explored landscape. The point of a synthesis is to stand as an authoritative statement for many years. The point of reconnaissance is to contribute provisionally to a continuing struggle for knowledge and democracy.

Reconnaissance is about generating knowledge outside conventional boundaries, rather than fortifying what we already know. It means taking risks that, generally, academics—who like to hang out in gangs and arm themselves with sharply worded footnotes—don't normally take. Yet part of this struggle for a new approach does necessarily involve something all too familiar to academia: the creation of new terms. This move can be defended only if it is necessary, and it is. We have to demonstrate, when we explore past socialisms, that we are not using the conventional, dated tool kit of the left. We are trying to put a somewhat familiar story, in other words, into a new framework—and to do that, the story itself has to be retold, in a new language.

First, it is useful in retelling the story of the Canadian left to think of those *matrix-events*—to borrow a useful term from the Annales school of French historians—that make specific leftisms conceivable. A matrix-event is a moment that reshapes hegemony at both its profoundest structural levels and its conscious levels. Capitalism and liberal order generate leftists routinely, because whole populations of people excluded from power and profits readily respond to critiques of their marginality. A mature liberal hegemony works to minimize the impact of this routine production of radicals. In the early twenty-first century I expect to hear global justice advocates denounce multinationals, social democrats push for public auto insurance, and environmentalists agitate against global warming—and these and other democratic radicals arrive, via the paths we've already described, in considerable numbers. Still,

I don't expect to see millions of people protesting on the streets of Toronto, the party structure collapsing in Ottawa, or the stock exchanges responding in panic to mass insurgency.

One point of reconnaissance is nonetheless to suggest that my expectation that the future will look much like the present, true in one pragmatic sense, is false in another. Most Canadians in 1926 would have had similarly limited expectations. Nothing that momentous seemed to be looming on the horizon. The few socialists and radicals among them, bedraggled after a half-decade of brutal labour wars, many of them defeats for the left, were as usual predicting a major economic and political crisis; and they were right. When evidence of an interwar economic crisis of capitalism became glaringly obvious with the stock-market crash, the Great Depression—a good example of a matrix-event—was on in earnest.

Marx's perception in *The Communist Manifesto* that capitalism routinely generates armies of radical activists and critics—its gravediggers—needs, then, to be made more historically specific to be useful to us today. Often it seems that only a very few misfits and malcontents—the usual radical suspects—are motivated to oppose the system. Then there are times and places when trickles turn into floods. There are events that transform the perceptions of life and the language of politics. These events alter, to some degree, the fundamental economic processes of society—the ways in which surplus value is extracted from labour, the family is reproduced and gender/sex roles determined, the state constituted and reconstituted, the nation imagined—and set in motion social and cultural processes of such a magnitude that they cannot be assigned to any one particular person or set of persons. They constitute times that rigorously test the quality of the left analysis and activism that preceded them.

An initial reconnaissance of the past hundred years or so of Canadian history reveals a number of matrix-events of enormous significance to the Canadian left. From the 1890s to 1910s, for instance, monopoly capitalism experienced a dramatic rise in its fortunes: a surge of mergers, cartels, and outright monopolies that transformed the social and economic landscape of much of North America. The locally owned, often family-owned, factory, mine, savings bank, or store suddenly seemed to be caught up in a massive centralization and consolidation of capital. Within a few decades big banks and corporations became hugely significant in the economy. This transformation set in motion a groundswell of agitation and writing on the "labour question"—which in 1901 held a certain status as the central issue of the hour, much as globalization does today. Many shared the conviction that a new science, "sociology," had emerged to explain patterns of social evolution. Many thinkers on both sides of the question agreed that corporate capitalism spelled the end of the individualistic political economy associated with Adam Smith. When capital's wars on the labour movement erupted with an astonishing violence from 1905 to 1913, overtly materialistic and Marxist approaches to reality attained a predominant influence throughout much of the left.[7]

The post-1914 collapse of the international order, exemplified by the Great War and, above all, the Russian Revolution, was another matrix-event—this one making it possible to "think socialism" as a real-world revolutionary possibility. Socialists drew connections between the two matrix-events. They related finance capital at home with imperialism and war abroad. A great postwar labour revolt swept up workers from coast to coast. The Winnipeg General Strike of 1919 and the Cape Breton coal wars of 1922–25 engraved themselves into long-term left memories. They were parts of a much larger pattern of unrest. These events radicalized an entire cohort of leftists who devoted the rest of their lives to fighting for a world revolution to end capitalism.[8]

Then came the Great Depression, resolved only by the advent of the Second World War. The Depression discredited liberal political economy as never before and prompted generations of Canadians to become proponents of state-planning. It created the preconditions of mass production, recognized trade unionism, and the culture of consumption—a combination that some scholars, loosely adapting Gramsci's work, call Fordism. The generation radicalized by this matrix-event would never yield in their belief in a planning state. To Fordism they responded with Radical Planism. Cradle-to-grave welfare provision; state planning for the economy; a massive expansion of public enterprise; a new Canadian nationalism: both Marx and John Maynard Keynes could be drawn upon to show that "democracy needs socialism."[9]

Yet another matrix-event was the post-1945 collapse of major European empires. The British and French cases were the most salient for Canadians. In the British case, Canada itself—already, as of 1931, a self-governing Dominion—underwent a wrenching economic and cultural transition. The echoes of the fall of the British Empire are still to be heard today in what is now a three-decades-long constitutional crisis in Canada and an unresolved Quebec question—one of the long-drawn-out and as yet unresolved national questions that have preoccupied many Canadians since the 1960s. In the French case, the collapse of French colonialism in Algeria and Indochina dramatized the world-historic significance of national liberation movements. The new dominant world power, the United States, would itself fight against the national liberation movement in Vietnam until the defeat of the U.S. forces in 1975. To live in this age was to live in a time when world capitalism seemed vulnerable to the rise of a totally different social system.[10]

The post-1960 rise of the women's movement—correlated with far-reaching changes in production and exchange, the advent of safe and accessible contraception and abortion, and a striking shift in the demographic composition of both the workplace and the trade unions—marks yet another Canadian matrix-event. What had once been called "the woman question" within socialism—why are women subordinate to men?—moved from a peripheral to a core concern, now that women rather than men assumed custody of "the question." The upshot of the women's revolution was a social transformation lived by many Canadians at the most personal level and a marked change in important state policies.

Since the 1980s something else that can be called a matrix-event has been unfolding: globalization. Ever-accelerating capital flows, the unprecedented industrial transformation of China and India, the collapse of space and time within a new cyber-capitalism, the creation of a global labour market, the ever more evident catastrophe of global environmental destruction, and the apparent diminution of the welfare state as an effective form of democratic resistance: all of these conditions are much-discussed post-Fordist symptoms of our own era. The next left will succeed to the extent that it shapes itself into a formation that provides important, and interrelated, answers to the challenges posed by these new conditions.[11]

In each case the matrix-event touched upon the most fundamental questions of how people survive and reproduce in a social order. Such convulsions are cyclical. Some would argue that they are related to well-documented rhythms of economic activity. Possibly—yet each in its magnitude and complexity defies any simplistic reduction to the business cycle. It is easier to see them coming in hindsight than it ever was to predict them. Their recurrence has given Marx-like ways of posing questions an enduring appeal quite separate from any particular application of his political ideas. Marx, above all a theorist of revolutionary change, is perennially found to be an important influence in rigorous discussions of the causation of such events. It is no great surprise that, long after the Communist Party declined to insignificance and the Soviet Union passed away, theorists of globalization are reading Marx with a new intensity. After all, "All that is solid melts into air," Marx said, and twenty-first-century social and economic theorists have picked up his observation and run with it.

The matrix-events all involved a palpable "shock of the new," and three of them were combined in such rapid succession from the 1930s to the 1970s that they created a palpable sense of a world turned upside down. Subtle, long-term transformations in economy and society manifested themselves in the lives of countless people as revolutionary changes in daily life. What had been common sense and merely part of life now seemed inexplicable and even unendurable. The very knowledge that it is possible to live otherwise—and that, if we don't do something, that "otherwise" may turn out to be something much worse than the future we desire—is part and parcel of that sense of heightened uncertainty and possibility that we might call "modernity."[12]

Wars and matrix-events often go together. In wartime the language of politics is transformed. Wars confront those asked to fight and support them with life-and-death issues. From the left, all the major wars that liberals have advocated and defended, with the exception of the Second World War, have revealed the emptiness of their hegemonic claim to represent the rational values of the Enlightenment. To an extent now forgotten, the Boer War (1899–1902) radicalized parts of the Liberal Party and propelled many middle-of-the-road Canadians into unimagined territories of left anti-imperialism. The First World War was widely denounced on the left as a carnival of the profiteers and ultra-imperialists. It also created—for the first time—an alliance of francophone nationalists and English-speaking leftists in a struggle against conscription. The craven failure of the liberal state to defend democracy in Spain in the 1930s stank in the nostrils of a left that dispatched some of its most idealistic members to fight the Fascists. The Second World War initially split the left. The Communist Party of Canada followed the Moscow Line; the CCF, apart from a few prominent leaders, supported the war. With the Nazi invasion of the Soviet Union in 1941, the left—at least officially—came together, although behind the scenes CCFers and CPCers battled each other in unions and organizations across the country. For many Canadians, the obvious success of the Canadian state in planning and building a massive industrial complex virtually out of nothing made the notion of a planned economy seem quite sensible. The Vietnam War hit Canadian leftists like a hammer blow, forcing even the most moderate into radical positions on Canadian independence and anti-imperialism. Throughout the twentieth century, "peace" has been the contested terrain on which much of the left has fought.[13]

A matrix-event taken in its broadest sense is a contradictory moment, generally located deep within the processes that structure society, outside the control of any individual, possibly extending over years—one that demands a new framework of understanding. Matrix-events send both apologists and critics of liberal order scrambling to understand what's happening and to craft effective responses. Such huge events generate scores of smaller, more localized versions of themselves. Take the evidence of our own times. "Globalization" is a much-debated abstraction. The layoff notice delivered to your desk or workbench announces a concrete event. The notice can be taken up, understood, and contained by the language of liberalism, with the outcome that those displaced by outsourcing come away with the message that it is up to them, as individuals, to reinvent themselves as workers. (A whole new industry advises those recently made redundant on how best to prepare themselves for the next of the many exciting careers they will pursue in life.) Or the notice can be taken up, understood, and contained by the language of democracy, with the outcome that those in this position see themselves as activists in a global struggle. What emerges from this moment over the much longer haul is not predetermined. When the system suddenly and strangely seems to generate anomalies and unprecedented injustices, the web of common sense and normality suddenly becomes visible.

For radicals and leftists, such specific occasions call out for great *moments of refusal.* A person suddenly sees through the order's appearance of permanence to its historical transience, through its politeness and orderliness to its underlying cruelty and violence, through its universality to its intransigent selectivity. People begin to talk out loud about the system's "unmentionable truths." In places like Seattle and Quebec City they begin to shout these truths to the world. At such moments, there is a widespread "speaking of bitterness." Masses of subalterns, hitherto silent or discreet, find their voices and shout their resistance, often, initially, in venerable vocabularies of outrage. In Canada as across North America, such moments are filled with spontaneous acts, at times violent, on the part of people who—quite suddenly—have just had enough.

One of the angriest of such moments of refusal occurred in the socio-economic crisis of the 1870s in the Maritimes. An acute international depression cut deeply into the lives of the mining and factory workers. People who had been enticed off their farms by the prospect of wage labour suddenly found themselves out of work. In Saint John, New Brunswick, a virtual civil war erupted: crowds of thousands in the street, and a violent, almost fatal assault upon a union-busting employer. On Cape Breton Island a mine manager complained about receiving anonymous letters threatening his livestock. Some of his restive, starving workers even fired a gun—some say a cannon—in his direction. In Londonderry, Nova Scotia, the steelworkers occupied their mill. In Springhill, after one wage cut too many, the workers secretly formed a association, which ultimately grew into a powerful coal-miners union that would eventually be home to many socialists. To these examples from the Maritimes we could add many more labour struggles all across the new Dominion. Apart from a few labour historians, who remembers them today? They were local, sporadic actions, separated off from any larger story; there was no party of socialism to inscribe them into a more general narrative and preserve their details; and so, dramatic as these moments of refusal were, they slipped out of popular historical memory.[14]

A sense of the intolerable does not wait upon a party to give it a manifesto. Often across Canada there are these moments of spontaneous defiance, of the *speaking of bitterness*: when bodies are thrown against the machine, when the personal becomes the political, when, bubbling irrepressibly up from the ranks of the insulted and the injured, we hear the voices saying, "No more! Enough is enough!" Better the "ruthless criticism of everything that exists" than compliance with such degrading conditions. Better, some of the Cape Breton miners of the 1870s must have believed, to threaten the mine boss with violence to his person (and his livestock) than meekly submit to his wage cuts. The difference between the nineteenth and the twentieth centuries is, basically, that in the later century organizations existed through which the memories of defiance could be preserved. In the twentieth century moments of spontaneous bitterness were often followed by *moments of supersedure* (to use an expression of Gramsci's). These are moments in which a person's understanding of the self and society, right and wrong, what really matters and what really doesn't, changes radically. Eley captures these moments well when he writes:

> In some periods and circumstances, the given relationships, socially and politically, seem inert and fixed. Culture signifies the predictable and overpowering reproduction of what "is". . . . Politics becomes the machinery of maintenance and routine. The image of a different future becomes displaced into fantasy and easily dismissed. . . . But at other times things fall apart. The given ways no longer persuade. The present loosens its grip. Horizons shift. History speeds up. . . . The expectations of a slow and unfolding habitual future get unlocked.[15]

You suddenly just "get it," you take up a new position in the world and break with the old. You could liken the moment of supersedure to the religious concept of epiphany. The social labyrinth is suddenly illuminated, the inadequacy of older maps is pitilessly exposed to the bright light, and new escape routes from suffering and entrapment emerge as plain as day. Suddenly you are lifted out of the realm of necessity, that passivity-generating, soul-destroying sphere, and—at least in your imagination, and sometimes in a marvellous actuality—transported into a realm of freedom where you can breathe the genuine, as opposed to formal-liberal, air of freedom. In these realms of freedom, a new form of life, a new socio-political order, a new spirit starts to take shape. The outlines of a new world, "rough and jagged though they always are," emerge in new morning; and they are—says Gramsci, in deeply moving reflections written in the prison cell provided for him by liberal-endorsed fascists—"better than the passing away of the world in its death throes and the swan-song that it produces."[16]

For the historian, always concerned to find reliable tests and checkable references, a good empirical indication of such a moment of supersedure is a sudden efflorescence of unauthorized grassroots writing. In such a time, radiant with the future, the radical presses blaze with energy: pamphlets, position papers, manifestos, broadsheets, letters, declarations stream from them, answering each other, creating—as if out of thin air—a new political universe. We find a round-the-clock cycle of meetings. For the people involved it becomes a matter of life or death to state their case before the tribunes of the world, and let the chips fall where they may.

In the years 1907–13, to take one early example, a torrent of words on evolutionary theory and socialist strategy poured from the presses. The socialist newspaper *Cotton's Weekly* from Quebec's Eastern Townships attracted as many as thirty thousand subscribers. Another example came in the early days of women's liberation in Canada, from 1969 to 1972, approximately, when tens of thousands of Canadian women spoke words of bitterness in consciousness-raising groups and lived and breathed the moment of supersedure. The Gestetner machines burned red-hot with their pamphlets. Homemade manifestos in Toronto were picked up within months in New York (and vice versa). Most every serious conversation was freighted with a revolutionary significance.

At such moments of supersedure the participants feel the urgency of sharing the new understanding with potential comrades. It shall be! It shall be! Or take francophone Montreal, 1965–72: a hundred groups, a thousand pamphlets, and in essence one overwhelming insight: enough is enough! A thousand people in movement nail their theses, hard-won from bitter experience, to the doors of the mighty, and they say: "Here we stand, we can do no other!" The participants urgently need to diffuse this new knowledge, to make it everybody's property, and—most importantly—to name and confront the Other whose rule, once seemingly so solid, now seems both contestable and contemptible. Down with them! The angry metaphors proliferate: crumbling foundations, rotting vegetation, wilful blindness, vicious gluttony, animalistic irrationality . . . the new dispensation arises, glorious and eloquent and terrible in an eruption of righteous anger. Get out of our way! Down with you! Demand the impossible! *À bas les anglais!* No more patriarchy! No more shit! Suddenly—in the words of the brilliant Canadian Marxist sociologist Dorothy Smith, speaking in the 1970s of the feminist moment of sisterhood—those so involved take up a "different location in the world."[17]

That white-hot moment soon fades, as white-hot moments always do, and some of those who were caught up in it are not strong enough to retain its memory. They too fade away and are lost to liberal order. They sink quietly back into the vast conformist mediocrity. They look back with fondness and patronage, or perhaps with a little embarrassment, at the realms of democratic freedom they once glimpsed. Others have committed their souls. They cannot lose the memory of a shaking and open world. They cannot forget the democracy they have fleetingly experienced.

There arrives, then, for those who remain—and to constitute a left formation, they must be numerous—the *moment of systematization*. The Great Refusal cedes place to a Strategic Withdrawal. The system did not fall, but its weaknesses are at least more apparent. Knowledge of its inner corruption, its banality, its knowing calculation of our weakness has not diminished a sense of radical opposition to it. If anything, watching how it picks off the weakest of the would-be radicals confirms the contempt of those leftists who remain. Radicals now devote themselves to the development of a specialized language. They look around the world for people undergoing similar struggles. They try to give the new knowledge a solid grounding in logic and evidence. Over time it all becomes a question of achieving a systematic understanding both of the moment of bitterness and the perceived need for an entirely new way of seeing. Gradually a new language of radicalism emerges. Gradually people try to connect their own first-hand experiences with the much larger world legacy of left struggle and resistance. Those who have undergone this experience aspire—in part because they have already invested so much of their lives—to become the leaders of all who would live otherwise.

This aspiration entails a hegemonic struggle within the left itself. It means that, just like their rulers, the ruled struggle to transcend their immediate economic and social interests, elaborate a common program in a language accessible to all of them, and—once their act is together—take their show on the road. Of decisive importance is the struggle both to name the oppressed and oppressors and make the new language of the left something that is spoken throughout civil society. This struggle has invariably meant a determined campaign against older idioms of resistance. The failings of older leftisms must be compared to the possibilities opened up by the new.

CONSTRUCTING FORMATIONS

The leftism that emerges from this systematization comprises a new philosophy, a new sociology (theoretical reflections on class, gender, nation, and so on), and a new set of institutions (or—but this is rare and seldom completely successful—the radical revision of old ones). The approach calls for a new utopianism, in the sense that Bauman gives us. Implicit, tentative, even shamefaced, with a thousand reservations, the new dispensation nonetheless requires a new and radiant future that will somehow redeem the bitter humiliations of the past and the onerous burdens of the present. It needs people to understand: "This is what it would *mean* to live, really live, otherwise!"

Even the most hard-talking, tough-minded, ruthlessly pragmatic leftists produce, between the lines, such projections of a possible future; and in constructing a *new otherwise*, they simultaneously produce a new present, a *historical present*: they inscribe each present-day struggle within a narrative stretching from the bitter past to the better future—rather than within the empty homogeneous space and time of capitalism, stretching pointlessly from one balance sheet and one business quarter into eternity.

Each of the Canadian left formations has had its own regional pattern. Canada is a markedly heterogeneous country, the second largest and most thinly populated on the planet. Most Canadians have at best a rudimentary knowledge of regions distant from their own home. Unsurprisingly, when they respond to waves of leftism, many of them emanating from distant parts, they do so in distinctive ways. Consider Calgary: today the heartland of the extreme right, but in the 1920s and 1930s a hotbed of radical movements and home to some of the country's most brilliant socialist theorists. (It is no coincidence that the first great meeting of the CCF was held in 1932 in Calgary, or that William Irvine, perhaps its most daring and consistent thinker, was a militant with the United Farmers of Alberta as much as he was a CCFer.) Conversely, a small library could be filled with patronizing depictions of the corruption and conservatism of the "backward" Maritimes, even from no less a socialist intellectual than the CCF's famous theoretician David Lewis. Now Halifax-Dartmouth and Northern New Brunswick figure among the more social-democratic districts in the country.

Often regional patterns were intensified by religious divisions. Throughout the entire period in which socialists built a movement in Canada, the largest single

Christian denomination was that of the Roman Catholics. They were, with minor exceptions, acutely suspicious of socialism as an atheism-in-disguise, a Bolshevik conspiracy, and a rival power. Until at least 1960, areas under strong Catholic influence—with some Cape Breton and Northern Ontario exceptions—were unlikely to provide good soil for socialism. Nowadays, with a Catholic Church that on economic questions can often sound more Marxist than the Marxists, and a Catholic population determined to make up its own mind on all matters political and moral, the situation has completely changed, and with it the regional pattern. Quebec, once seen, like the Maritimes, as immemorially conservative, is now the undisclosed guarantor of much of the Canadian parliamentary left, for the sovereigntist MPs it sends to Ottawa in such numbers are generally social-democratic nationalists suspicious of U.S.-inspired foreign policies. Many people outside Quebec now see in its publicly funded day-care program a model that Canada as a whole might take up, rather as leftists in the 1960s looked to Saskatchewan's prototype of public medicine.

One way of "talking socialism" may resonate in one region and with some people and not others. In the early twentieth century, for example, a hard-hitting materialistic speech on socialism that drew upon the labour theory of value might have had more appeal for an audience of coal-miners in Nanaimo than the same presentation would have had for an audience of reform-minded Methodist clergymen in Toronto. In the 1960s only some people in some places warmed up to left rhetoric that drew upon the metaphors of national liberation and independence. For others, the very same figures of speech called into question the pan-Canadian state-building project they had learned to equate with leftism. Rather than thinking in terms of essences—reactionary Quebec, the conservative Maritimes, dowdy Ontario, the populist Prairies, unpredictable British Columbia—it seems much more useful to think of radical unevenness and changing social patterns *within* generally acknowledged regions.

No left organization operates in a vacuum. None ever has "the left" all to itself. (Even the very first socialists had to share the left with radical Liberals and social reformers of various descriptions.) What each left organization seeks to build is a *formation*, a way of disseminating its system of concepts through a much wider social network. A successful formation—or "historic bloc," following Gramsci—is a collective agent in history (the "Jacobins" in the French Revolution, or the socialist feminists in 1970s North America, for example) that has successfully undergone a moment of systematization and hence is able to intervene effectively in the historical process. In a social and economic world that often seems to be mechanically deterministic, a historic bloc enjoys at least some room to manoeuvre. Its very understanding of the structuring forces in history allows it, although always only to a certain extent, to go beyond those forces. A left formation is a historic bloc in emergence—an attempt to transcend the iron logic of economic and social determinism ("base and superstructure" in conventional parlance) by the formation of a new historical agent, a complex unity made up of unique individuals amidst contrasting and even contradictory social forces, but united by an overriding political objective—that of reasoning and living otherwise. Each formation is, in its period of dominance, "that section which pushes forward all others" on the left.[18] It might have a "party" (in the conventional sense) at its core; it might have several parties; or it might have none.

Conceiving of left history in terms of formations suggests that parties, individuals, and events, all important topics calling out for serious inquiry, are best understood as moments in a larger process of becoming. This position marks a distinct departure from a vertical history approach. For example, the conventional (whether anti-Communist or Marxist-Leninist) approach to the narration of the history of communism assumes that, from the Bolshevik Revolution to 1989, "communists" were pretty much all birds of a feather. They were proponents of the revolutionary overthrow of capitalism and critics of social democrats (located to their "right"), who favoured parliamentary gradualism. If you are a Marxist-Leninist, you establish that the post-1917 advent of a real party identifying with the revolution marks the beginning of the history of the entire movement. If you are a critic of the Marxist-Leninists, you establish that the emergence of the Communist Party in 1921 was a tragic and divisive mistake. Then you argue your positions out, in polemical texts and poisonous footnotes, for the remainder of your lives. For both sets of historians the task is to write a vertical narrative that tracks the Communist Party—wondrous breakthrough or weird breakdown, depending on your point of view—from earliest days to the present.

The unconventional (horizontal) approach I recommend would pay far more attention to how, after 1917, a Bolshevik left formation gradually consolidated itself, provisionally uniting very different sets of radicals largely through the widespread appeal of the Russian Revolution. Thus one did not have to be a communist to be deeply influenced by the Bolshevik formation. A man like J.S. Woodsworth, who came to socialism primarily via the path of a spiritual critique of capitalism, could nonetheless see the importance of publishing in the Communist press and travelling, as one of a succession of well-disposed pilgrims, to see socialism first-hand in the Soviet Union. After this Bolshevik left formation had had its day, after 1937 or so, communists could, while ostensibly wholly faithful to Bolshevik legacy, in fact become much more like the social democrats they had earlier so criticized. Stewart Smith, author of a fire-breathing denunciation of the CCF as "social fascist" in the early 1930s, devoted his time in that decade's closing years to devising solutions to such non-revolutionary problems as planning the pattern of one-way streets in downtown Toronto. In other words, understanding the implications of the words "communist" and "social democrat" means knowing the context in which they are used. No doubt, becoming a Socialist Party member, Social Democrat, Communist, CCFer, Péquiste, or Feminist Party supporter could mark a milestone in a person's life. Such parties were significant actors, and vertical histories that study such affiliations play a useful role. But they would be all the more informative if the horizontal conditions of ideological context and cohort are taken into account—and it is in illuminating these conditions that the concept of formation can play a constructive role.

The left formations may share many words and even concepts with each other, yet they rely on conceptual and political systems that assign meaning to these words and concepts in different ways. Think of a deck of playing cards. Each card within the deck is a discrete material and symbolic entity—it has a vertical, free-standing, even objective (in the sense of generally understood and shareable) identity. The Queen of Spades is the Queen of Spades—you and I can probably both call up the image of the card in our minds. Yet within a given game each and every card also derives its meaning from the horizontal context of the game itself. The Queen of Spades is an extraordinary card in the game of Hearts, and just one more face card in Gin Rummy. In moving from that analogy to history, we have to imagine "games" that are in fact matters of life and death. The "cards" are concepts, references, memories, symbols, and actions that, within one formation, are taken to be absolutely pivotal to any authentic and serious left. Within another they may be completely secondary or even of no importance. From the sectarian point of view, a common approach to those within another left formation is simply to dismiss their seriousness and their intelligence—*their* leftism is childish and unreal, whereas *ours* is realistic and valid. *We* don't recognize *their* markers—we may not even be able to see them. The alternative strategy that I recommend is to study the content of each formation by always remembering the *context* within which this *content* was elaborated—by analogy, the game within which the card was played.

The very intensity with which the left experiences its history can mean that it lives that history in a particular and seemingly inescapable way. There rarely appears to be a non-partisan possibility of truth in these moments of historical reinvention. Each formation has constructed a (generally implicit) framework that allows for discrimination between true and false statements. Each has evolved a "politics of the truth." Each formation has developed from Marx, and then added from other sources, the elements of a systematic sociology. In so doing, it has also dialectically transformed this sociology, as it integrates a more and more subtle understanding of the society that it has studied in all its peculiarities.

Each left formation organizes a conceptual system, which—at the limit—comes to be defended as an integrated science. Such a system provides categories through which the world can be logically understood and actions in the present connected with possible future outcomes. It allows partisans to discriminate between the "real" and the "unreal," the "true" and the "false," the "we" and the "them." Of special significance to historians is how the formation names the Other against which the left is to organize, because how carefully this Other is named will have a direct bearing on how the formation conceptualizes and acts upon the concept of Us. There will be a new *practice* of leftism, political and cultural, that both reflects this new understanding and—as categories and descriptive terms are repeated over and over again—constructs and reconstructs it, day after day.

At least in theory, and often in practice, the formal organizations—parties, unions, various groupings—related to the formation bear some resemblance to its system of concepts. So too do the less conspicuous, but perhaps no less important, cultural organizations—summer camps, newspapers, study groups—wherein the formation attempts to distil its insights and communicate them to adherents and sympathizers. Each left formation has historically identified the upbringing and education of children as a particularly important sphere of struggle for the left, and it appears to be a symptom of the confidence of a left formation if it actively creates institutions and programs designed to mould the next generation.

Each formation also provides for the education of its adult members—some involving highly ambitious publication programs. Each formation has its concepts of gender roles and permissible sexuality. Each has a "style of life" appropriate to its adherents, but which also excludes those outside the circle. Each has its own characteristic dialect of a more general language of leftism: many key terms used within one formation (God, class, justice, comrade, sister) either mean something different in another, or may not even "signify" at all. Each formation celebrates some authorities (or a specific approach to the figures that it shares with others), and implicitly marginalizes others. Each requires—certainly for its leaders, if not for every follower—familiarity with certain foundational texts. Some texts will be shared with the left as a whole—here Marx has traditionally figured as an important unifier—but will be read in a particular way. Others will be distinctive to the formation itself, and unknown outside it.

Each formation generates a strong feeling of belonging. Young activists are required to make a large investment in time and energy in the "symbolic political capital" that the formation offers. They will eventually fight hard, against other leftists as well as liberals, to defend this investment against devaluation. At the same time these same young activists may have a psychological need to slaughter their elders, to emerge on the "stage of history" as masters rather than apprentices. Within every formation in Canada there have been struggles that suggest a conflict between generations.

A formation must, at a minimum, generate new sites and new strata of resistance. There must be entities that preserve the memory of supersedure—newspapers, books, films, television programs, and (these days) web-sites. A formation generates many different kinds of "spaces," both figuratively and literally. It creates spaces in which the formation's texts are generated—collectives, editorial board rooms, plenary sessions. It creates spaces in which the formation struggles to create and preserve a sense of community—national society halls, club rooms. It creates spaces in which the young are shaped—summer camps, day cares, youth clubs. It creates other spaces in which its memories are preserved and a sense of history commemorated—cemetery sites, anniversary celebrations, obituaries. Each formation has its own imagined international geography through which it positions its participants in the world. (Often its principle of hope requires that it identify a place on the globe where the realm of freedom has unequivocally arrived.) At first most Canadian formations import their leftism almost holus bolus from other places. Over time they adjust their balance of trade with the external world. Strategies of merely reprinting foreign news and feting foreign figures give way to homegrown efforts and the creation of domestic intellectuals.

We learn we are in the presence of a new formation when large numbers of leftists—often a cohort drawn from the same generation—start naming new problems and using new words to announce a radical break with existing reality. Some of the best evidence of the existence of this new language may come from the new formation's opponents, acting as so many leukocytes announcing the presence of a new infection. There is a "shared language of socialism," in historian Gerald Friesen's words.[19] Within this shared language are many different dialects. A cohort does not require unanimity, and indeed may be riven by fierce divisions. What it does require is a shared and distinctive system of concepts, implicit or explicit, that a historian can recover from the evidence. To make the case that a given formation exists, we must at a minimum be able to show that it involved a particular reading of history and that it entailed distinctive practices, institutions, and causes that functioned as a kind of "planetary system" around the new conceptual sun announced by its moment of supersedure. If participants embrace the conceptual system that shapes the formation, they see totality through its categories. If they are more loosely within the orbit of the formation, it exerts a subtler but still noticeable influence.

Each leftist in each formation stands under the injunction to become an intellectual. Many, of course, do not really do so; they fit themselves into the formation as agitators, organizers, rank-and-file members. Nonetheless: the way in which they agitate and organize and belong is shaped itself by the formation and by the conceptual system at its heart. You might well join the Communist Party in the 1930s simply to organize an effective union in the steel mill, but you would not last long in the Party (at least not down to 1937) if you expressed absolutely no interest in the works of Lenin or went to sleep in rallies designed to inspire sympathy with the Republicans in the Spanish Civil War. You might well join the Rassemblement pour l'indépendance nationale to impress your peers at the Université de Montréal, but you would probably not last long in the party if you were visibly uninterested in Quebec's independence or bored by the whole knotty question of the primacy of socialism or nationalism.

Leftists have traditionally been—and, I am tempted to say, by definition always are—haunted by spectres from the past. They are "non-contemporaneous" with themselves, insofar as they have internalized a sense of being involved in a process of history that extends long before, and will endure long after, their individual lifetimes. They are not "all there," in the present, because they are in their minds living as much in the past and in the future. Even in the most day-to-day activities, they carry with them the idea of the more general historical pattern into which these activities fit. This intense historicism means that each left formation comes to live its history in an intense, partisan, and inescapable way. A given group within a given cohort will reinvent the radical tradition, and over time this becomes a significant barrier to communication across an increasingly variegated community. When the truth becomes wholly partisan, the formation has passed its years of creative development, because it can neither verify or falsify its formulations nor readily communicate them to others.

One of the easiest ways to tell when one left formation has given away to another is when you see a sudden transformation of "narrative line." Just as a brilliant card in one game may not even be involved in another game, a historical event that radiates significance and portends the future within one formation may have no role whatever to play within the next. For example, major historical events such as the Cape Breton or Vancouver Island coal wars of the first quarter of the twentieth century had nothing to say that was particularly interesting to socialist feminists of the 1970s and 1980s. They pertained to what was described as a "male left," and not to the new formation's narrative of human liberation. Nor did they have much significance within CCF-NDP narratives, wherein the coalminers were conceptualized as impoverished victims calling out for adult education rather than as working-class intellectuals powering the revolutionary left.

At any given moment, even as it addresses itself to the burning issues of the day, a formation entails a delicate balance between invented traditions and imagined futures. As much as it lives and breathes in the past, each socialist formation will also prefigure radically different futures. All are in Bauman's sense utopian in struggling to organize futures that are radically otherwise, although these socialist futures run the gamut from modern societies operating with the efficiency of giant machines to decentralized collectivities working on the basis of producers' self-management. Every formation has wrestled with the fundamental question of how to make its vision "real" in an often indifferent world. How do members bring into the mainstream a movement whose conceptual breakthrough and relationship with past and present require a radical disengagement from, in fact a scathing and damning critique of, the surrounding socio-political order? How, drawing on Alain Touraine's vocabulary, do members go from "identity," the recognition of a shared condition, to "opposition," the claiming of a position of struggle, to "totality," the alternative rationality of the movement—the movement's particular challenge to the dominant worldview?[20] Or how, to use more Gramscian terminology, do enthusiasts wage a long-term war of position that preserves the moments of supersedure and systematization without succumbing to the co-optive strategies of liberal passive revolution? How do you convert the events of everyday life into a cumulative struggle for a life that is truly otherwise—that really is an anticipation of a very different future? How does one movement unite with others to form a historic bloc—a left formation that is not, properly understood, just an "alliance" but a collective actor capable of refashioning the very economic and social bases from which it has risen? How can this historic bloc prefigure a realm of freedom, when it must also fight for everyday demands and even for its life? How do you keep the dream of freedom alive, in a world that demands a constant and compromising engagement with its specific necessities?

ESTABLISHING THE TERRAIN

A country's leftism is inseparable from the structures it is trying to change. Understanding the history of a left tradition within any particular framework requires (to borrow and translate remarks by French sociologists

Daniel Becquemont and Laurent Mucchielli) a preliminary inventory of the terrain on which the imported framework is supposed to work: its points of unity and division, its intellectual, social, and political dynamics, its symbols.[21] No matter with what force of conviction a leftism is propounded, it is illusory to think that it is intervening in a brand-new intellectual space. Understanding "the party of the left" in Canada means grasping the challenges that leftists have confronted when they tried to make their ideas, often derived from outside the country, effective within the context of the liberal project that is Canada.

Many of the existing histories of the left misrepresent the challenge confronted by such leftists. They often go overboard, one way or the other. Some treat Canadian radicals in isolation from the world. Many of the histories of the CCF-NDP go down this line. They typically begin with the Great Depression, move on to the radical clergymen and middle-class intellectuals who were against the sufferings caused by that Depression, and conclude with an all-Canadian roster of electoral events and provincial governments. The CCF-NDP, we are left to assume, was a party that applied made-in-Canada solutions to Canadian problems. These studies look at a figure like J.S. Woodsworth and focus intensively on the homegrown influences—crises within Methodism, his own first-hand observations of the conditions of immigrants in Winnipeg and later of the Winnipeg General Strike of 1919, his pacifism-cum-isolationism through the 1930s—as aspects of the man understandable without reading much beyond Canadian borders. Certainly the "made-in-Canada" theme predominates in the official histories of the New

Democratic Party, the descendant of the CCF. What tends to be radically underplayed in such treatments is the immensely powerful influence of British and U.S. socialist thinkers at crucial junctures in the party's history, and the significant, continuing influence of Marx. The intellectual history of the CCF, for example, would have been very different without the Rhodes Scholars who cut such proud figures in the League for Social Reconstruction and in the party more generally. A list of external influences on the CCF could be extended almost indefinitely.[22]

Other histories go down the opposite path. They assume that the leftists were just the local subservient franchise-holders of an international radical brand name. The Communist Party of Canada often seemed like, and has been described as, little more than a passive recipient of Moscow directives. Certainly in the years following 1928 (when the Communists became more and more integrated into the workings of the Communist International) or 1932 (when the Comintern papers suggest a clamping down on the Canadian party), the description matches up with important parts of reality. Yet, characteristically, radical formations in Canada change over time. They start off by borrowing massively from other countries. Their heroes, pivotal texts, big debates are all imported. Then, after a decade or so, as a cohort grows into its time and place, the formation changes. It starts to generate interesting idiosyncrasies that set it apart on the world stage. One of the peculiarities of the Canadians is that, while they often seem to be simply following British, U.S., and French trends, they just as often discreetly adapt them to suit their own purposes. The Canadian political and social situation resembles, but it is not the same as, that of other countries. Since Maurice Spector's pathbreaking work that attempted to define Canada's world position in the mid-1920s, thereafter deeply controversial within the Communist Party, it has been important for every major formation to develop a position on the national question. Does the projected left-wing Canada include Quebec? Does a left-wing Quebec remain in Canada? Do leftists speak for the First Nations? For racial minorities? If not, what should the relationship be? What is Canada—an imperialist power that the left should oppose, a colonized country that the left should liberate, or some perplexing hybrid of the two? A history of the Communists that slighted this internal debate would be missing important nuances of the theme of external domination.

From the beginning of Canadian socialism, socialists have argued that to construct a new post-liberal social order will require "a new philosophy of life, a new culture," to cite one Canadian leftist from 1911.[23] They have tried to put together conceptual frameworks that do useful work in the world, illuminate a situation, identify core problems. How they assembled these frameworks, the intelligence and discernment brought to their construction and deployment, determined how well analysis could guide political action and how effective, over the long term, that political action would be. It is both necessary and difficult to survey existing bodies of expertise and decide which elements can be effectively incorporated into a counter-hegemonic dynamic.

Still, if many concepts were simply conscripted from the surrounding society without careful reflection on how they might fit within a new counter-hegemonic logic, participants could easily wind up with a slightly eccentric, left-sounding version of the dominant ideology. A "magpie leftism" roams the globe in search of shiny new theories and eloquent heroes, but it spends little time worrying about whether these theories jibe with each other or whether these heroes are really talking the same language. Conversely, a "bald-headed eagle leftism" soars above the landscape, occasionally zeroing in on some hapless bourgeois rabbit, but magnificently disconnected from the grubby provincial world of Canada unfolding below. Interestingly, although the eagles certainly cut a much more romantic figure than the magpies, they are just as vulnerable to the earthly (horizontal) environmental changes at work far beneath them. If you rigorously refuse any dealings with bourgeois society, with the social groups that history suggests have often been drawn to the left, and with the mundane business of getting your message across, you will end up with your voice calling out only to the wind. A particular leftism can work to provide its devotees with a "filter" of specialized words and images so thick that nothing from the external world can raise any profound questions about its conceptual system's fruitfulness as a guide to social reality. Such purity comes at a cost. If all room is eliminated for any test of key representations against the goal of realizing a realm of freedom, the formation has started to become a historical artifact rather than a history-making force. It has started speaking only to itself, defending a set of doctrines that forbid any questions. It is on the road to a cult-like irrelevance.

Even if members within a formation manage to find a politics of truth that allows for a test of practice, a further debate remains: who decides, and using what measure, how the test is specified and whether or not it has been passed? As Sue Golding insightfully remarks, from Marx forward there has been a problem "of connecting the ethical assumptions inherent in the search for, and attempts to establish, a better or progressive or more democratic society, without presupposing an *a priori* or metaphysical given or ignoring the specificity of history in creating that (or any other) meaning." Each formation, she adds, "must take seriously Marx's claim that *history*, and not abstract thought, delineates the foundation and terrain upon which people are able to understand their circumstances and change them for the better."[24]

If we position each socialist formation against the liberal order that it seeks simultaneously to subvert, preserve, and transform, we can begin to measure up to this challenge. We can evaluate each one as an experiment in living otherwise. Did the formation change people's lives? How? Did it change the Canadian political order? Did it leave behind models and texts that proved useful within other formations? What were the formation's advantages and disadvantages? This may seem like a rather obvious way of looking at the topic, but few writers have taken it up. It is as if, instead of doing this kind of work, we are more accustomed to signing up in our imaginations as members of, or enemies of, the formation in question, rather than taking several steps back and looking at it from a standpoint, at once both sceptical and sympathetic, that assumes both the value and the difficulty of projecting realms of freedom into a particular period of time.

Inspired often by matrix-events that they have internalized and that generate moments of supersedure that, even if momentarily, reveal underlying contradictions in the social order, leftists in a given formation will struggle to elaborate a new conceptual system. Many will attempt to "reverse" the bourgeois discourses around them, trying to hold them up to their own standards, and play them back against themselves. They will articulate their system of concepts in ways that try to address potential sympathizers where they find them. They will work out and apply sociologies of Canada and the "subject-positions" that are implied by them—like "the worker" or "women for peace" or "the peace-loving Canadian" or "sisters." They will look for ways of giving shape and system to the moment of supersedure that they strive to honour and to perpetuate.

The risks of rethinking Canadian leftisms this way are not negligible. For one thing, we would ultimately change the subject(s) of the history of the Canadian left, to encompass a far greater diversity of people—those of religious and cultural figures, the First Nations and visible minorities, feminists and environmentalists, Quebec nationalists, among others—whose words and deeds can be linked implicitly or explicitly to a post-liberal democratic future. This is a more complicated business than narrating the history of a party (not that we don't need more of that). We are trying to get at, not just the institutions, but at the shifting *mentalités* of large groups of people. One risk of this is, of course, to turn everyone into an intellectual—even activists who are primarily engaged in the day-to-day work of the left. Empirically, we can demonstrate that very often activists were keenly involved in left-wing intellectual life. You could fill a large auditorium with hundreds of people in Halifax in 1920 for a debate about capitalism and the labour theory of value. Well-circulated newspapers like the *Western Clarion* and *Cotton's Weekly* critically analyzed scores of Western intellectuals with enthusiasm. For over forty years the labour writer Colin McKay brought his readers analyses of Hegel, Spencer, and Marx, along with commentaries on more down-to-earth issues agitating the left. The legendary Cape Breton radical J.B. McLachlan could quote Thomas Carlyle and Robert Burns whenever his argument called for them. The words of John Ruskin, the British art critic and philosopher, echoed in the majestic utopian writings of the brilliant prairie visionary E.A. Partridge. Granting some points to the thesis that "mass culture" damaged this proud tradition of self-taught radicalism, I think leftists should also remember warnings advanced by writers in cultural studies against putting too much stock in "hypodermic needle" models of cultural history, whereby hapless consumers are rendered by advertising and other noxious influences into passive victims. One of the most impressive lessons of the feminist revolution was to demonstrate the zeal for radical insight that could be awakened within a subaltern group patronizingly dismissed as know-nothings. Countless self-taught environmental activists today, who regularly go head to head with the hired guns of the corporate polluters, serve as another example. Politically, a leftism that imagines that every member of the movement has the intelligence to respond critically and creatively to his or her environment is to be preferred to one that converts its members into "transmission belts" conveying messages from the central committee to the marginal members.

TOWARDS A MODEL-BUILDING AGENDA

Reconnaissance does not, in and of itself, definitively settle the issue of cultural autonomy, or indeed other issues. It does provide information—sightings and correlations—open to empirical confirmation and falsification. Such an analytical reconstruction can probably never, in and of itself, attain the solidity of a science or, conversely, the vividness and intimacy of a memoir. A reconnaissance is not a trial by jury but a first attempt to map a terrain. Reconnaissance sees the historian's job to be not one of calling each leftism up before the Bar of History and deciding whether its partisans should be praised or damned (there is a vast library of books, especially U.S., that can be consulted for those who enjoy this Cold War genre) but rather one of understanding how each worked as a system of thought and structure of activism for the people involved in it.

This way of writing the history of the left removes three conventional safety nets. The first to go is the safety net of the "ironic" or "tragic" narrative style, much beloved by contemporary historians impressed with their own omniscience and their superiority to the subjects of history. Each socialism was an experiment in post-liberal democratic politics. Each merits a detailed and careful reconstruction. The liberal ironist imagines past leftists as the naive butts of the joke of the master ironies of history, whose master narratives he has disposed of. (That the tale of this "great escape" from the master narrative is itself a master narrative escapes him or her.) A socialist reconnaissance respects such leftists as co-investigators in a continuing democratic project, upon which much continues to depend.

Reconnaissance also means renouncing the safety net of writing only about people or movements closely associated with oneself. In the past, Communists or their sympathizers have generally been those who wrote Communist history; social democrats wrote on the CCF-NDP; Quebec nationalists wrote about the Quebec liberation struggle; feminists wrote about socialist feminism; gays about gay liberation. There are sound reasons why those who pretend to "speak for" minorities to which they do not belong have been warned against trespassing and appropriation of voice. It is presumptuous of men to speak of women, of tenured professors to speak of industrial workers, or of women to speak of gay men, if doing so implies an implied right either to "speak for" the interests of the other or to intuit and then write authoritatively about his or her heartfelt experiences. Reconnaissance makes no claims to speak on behalf of the people it describes and contextualizes. This is not its province. (When, as is necessarily sometimes the case, it deduces consciousness from behaviour, it must proceed with utmost caution.) A mission of reconnaissance is inherently an exercise in trespassing—breaking boundaries and developing in-depth knowledge of hidden terrain—for the purpose of contributing to a more general understanding. What each socialism has left for us is a corpus of texts. These can be reconstructed in terms of their content and form—to show how they worked in the world. Some plausible inferences can be made about how people wanted them to work in the world and about the audiences assumed by these texts. In rare moments we can actually document how a given text was received. But the souls of the leftists, especially those materialists who fiercely denied having souls, are inaccessible to us.

The third missing safety net is that of shaping the account around institutions that everybody knows were or are important. Here a sense of security resulted from using a commonly accepted chronology of generally accepted important events. Such events survive in reconnaissance, but—like our friend the Queen of Spades—they now play a different role. Reconnaissance asks: "What was the institution trying to do, and how did it try to do it? How skilfully did the group/party/newspaper/caucus/organization speak the dialect of socialism it was dedicated to developing?" What reconnaissance does not provide is any reassurance that institutions in themselves offer us the "turning points" or the "benchmarks" of history. A poem may be as revealing as a party; a newspaper of greater moment than an election.

If we define a socialist formation as an emergent historic bloc, a complex unity made up of unique individuals, contrasting and even contradictory social forces, using its own dialect of a shared language of socialism and its own distinctive way of crafting a relationship between past and future in present-day politics: if we do all that, we are still left with some concrete questions about how to put this heuristic device to work. One obstacle to remove is that of wishful thinking. I think there should be such a formation as "queer leftism" in Canada. I think one could mobilize a language of leftism oriented to the ideal of liberating sexual minorities. I can even think of a pantheon of ancestors, from Oscar Wilde (so rarely studied as a socialist figure) on the international level to dozens of prominent Trotskyist and neo-Marxist activists throughout North America who took up gay liberation from the 1960s to the 1980s, often incurring ridicule (and even expulsion) for their pains. I can see on the horizon of critical democratic theory a substantial number of queer theorists who have reconfigured gender politics over the past decade. Nonetheless, a few dozen swallows do not a springtime make. "Queer leftism" is a hopeful projection into the future, not a historically significant counter-hegemonic formation that can be documented in Canadian left history. "Formations" in the sense I mean the term here attracted or influenced thousands of people, generated hundreds of publications, and created long-lasting and large institutions, libraries, archives, and literatures. They constructed substantial and sustained critical movements, usually lasting for more than two decades. They were emergent historic blocs, which succeeded—to an extent and for a time—in transcending the iron cage of base and superstructure to form a new historical agent, a complex unity made up of unique individuals, united by an overriding political objective.

Another challenge of reconnaissance comes in assessing a formation's period of strength and weakness. One formation did not replace another cleanly, with the ultimate last one standing. Rather, each formation, while analytically distinct, necessarily involved a complex intermingling and overlapping with other approaches. Membership statistics of parties and organizations and voting statistics are at best helpful proxies. An especially revealing indication is whether activists not well integrated into a formation nonetheless feel obliged to "speak its language" and appear in its media.

Later formations often claim to have fully absorbed and transcended the achievements of their predecessors. They will even attempt to lay claim retrospectively to some of their leading figures. They will more judiciously learn from them, even while declaring their rivals utterly superseded. To make the historical analysis of formations yet more complicated, leftists are notorious for changing their minds, all the while stoutly denying that they have done so. They move from one party to another, and from one formation to another, perhaps even volubly protesting their 100 per cent ideological consistency. Thus while each formation has its own moment of flourishing, its own time when it seems to contemporaries to articulate the deep-seated contradictions of the system and the means to overcome them, all "periodizing hypotheses" have to be approximate and are open to debate. Moreover, to complicate things still further, it is always possible to revive a formation, to "reinvent tradition" as it were—although, in my opinion, such reinventions have usually had a certain nine-day-wonder unreality about them. Nothing was more typical of the late 1970s and early 1980s, for example, than romantic reinventions of the Communist International's Third Period of the early 1930s, revivals that for a time and in places did really generate considerable commitment and enthusiasm for the latter-day "New Communists."

Cohorts do take up a given set of ideas and practices at a given moment, but the formation they construct, if it is successful, will have some influence beyond its average heyday of twenty-five years. Long after they packed Toronto's Maple Leaf Gardens for a massive rally in 1934, the Communists were still a force to be reckoned with in parts of the Canadian left (for example, in many major unions and in the peace movement). Long after the great protest marches and university occupations of the late 1960s and early 1970s, New Left ideas could still be heard on university campuses. A further complication: while formations can be tied, loosely, to given periods, they overlap: and in overlapping, they influence each other.

Given that all historically significant Canadian leftisms have engaged with "Marx," no matter how fiercely they argued with each other leftists could always conduct their debates in a familiar language. Many texts of Marx have been read as road maps to the realm of freedom, humanity's conscious and collective ability to make decisions over economic and social forces. This Marxist stance on freedom entails four further positions: the critique of the class content and pretensions to universal significance of classical liberalism; the development of historical materialism, which emphasizes the class-determined and economically dependent nature of human ideals, within socio-economic systems that are not freely chosen; the articulation of a possible "outside" to such restrictions, in a "kingdom of freedom," wherein the human species would be liberated "from the blind forces of the market" and the restraints of private property; and the elaboration of a holistic philosophy of history that combines historical materialism with a vision of the realization of freedom, that is, the fulfilment of humanity's potential nature, a "mode of existence in which humans are integrated and self-determining." "Marx's ideal of the emancipation of humankind," one author remarks, "was essentially different from the liberal ideal of individual freedom, both in its 'old liberal' and in its 'new liberal' versions."[25] That all Canadian formations to date have been influenced to varying degrees by this ideal is a matter of great interest.

Unlike earlier and later versions of particular sciences—astrology and astronomy, say—the conceptual systems of left formations share common terms and empirical reference points. Formations do not entail absolutely untranslatable languages, completely distinct bodies of knowledge. A leftist of 1905 and a leftist of 2005 could hold a conversation, cite at least some of the same texts (even if in different translations), and express many of the same critiques of the liberal bourgeoisie and capitalist society. And yet—if I am right—the leftist of 2005 would find the outlook of the socialist of 1905 difficult to endorse, not just because of the details of a particular political position, but because of the underlying system of concepts used to justify it. For example, within the socialism hegemonic on the left in 1905, the subordination of women to men was conceptualized within a neo-Darwinist theory of social evolution that interpreted "men" and "women" as self-evident natural phenomena. Similarly, "races" existed as actually existing entities—even historical forces with memories and interests. Radical sexual politics entailed questioning monogamy and promoting contraception, but often in terms of sustaining the long-term health of "the race." Leftists could unselfconsciously love the writings of Jack London, Rudyard Kipling, and Charlotte Perkins Gilman, all writers seen as racist today, and some of the most articulate could buy into theories of eugenics—the notion that society should consciously influence (and in some versions, much less supported on the left, dictate) the reproductive choices of individuals so that the "fittest" survived and the "degenerates" disappeared.

From the standpoint of 2005, educated as it has been by socialist feminism and queer theory, these positions would not only be hard to defend, but also difficult even to express within the dominant vocabulary of the left. A leftist today who proclaimed herself devoted to the "interests of the white race" would probably encounter more than a little scepticism, and one who praised eugenics might find it hard to find an enthusiastic audience even in the Conservative Party in Calgary (where eugenics-based legislation on compulsory sterilization of the supposedly unfit was on the books until the 1970s). In short, much of what the Canadian left had to say about gender and sexuality in 1905, for all the attempts to root its statements in evolutionary theory, would seem politically offensive, intellectually threadbare, and hardly "leftist." As a gay man, I found it personally disheartening to find this vocabulary of degeneration and fitness still up and running in the 1970s—a time when some Toronto leftists spoke quite freely about "faggots" and elsewhere Trotskyists earnestly debated about whether or not they should relax long-standing policies of expelling their homosexual comrades—and the temptation is simply to reach for words like "homophobia," "intolerance," and "sexism."

Yet as a Gramscian I find such a personal response intellectually and politically deficient. It fails what I might call the "Golding test"—the test of trying not to impose on the history of the left an "*a priori* or metaphysical given" and "ignoring the specificity of history in creating that (or any other) meaning."

It is not only more interesting, but more politically useful, to look at those leftists of 1905 (and of 1975) with a compassionate as well as critical eye, to reconstruct the underlying reasons as to why they talked and acted a certain way, why they highlighted some issues that seem minor to us and disparaged other issues that today seem so central. Leftists in 2105 who look back at leftists in 2005 are undoubtedly going to face the same challenge. They will ask themselves—"How could they have used such a vocabulary? Missed such an obviously important issue? Talked in such an unselfconsciously ___ist way?" If they are creative, they will not just reach for their (presumably amply restocked) vocabularies of dismissal, but struggle to understand what it was that made us tick. That will make for better history and a more self-aware, critical, and responsible left politics.

Similarly, for all the ink that has flowed on the absolute differences between Communists and CCFers—to take a leading example from Canadian left history—it seems to me that a Communist of the 1940s and a CCFer of the 1940s shared a hierarchy of key problems and a mutually understandable language in which they could express their disagreements. I think they were both playing a language game in which the mighty "Queen of Spades" was "The Plan." Most likely they would both unselfconsciously admire many aspects of the Soviet Union, and debate whether or not it was a people's democracy. Such a shared system of concepts did not mean a "happy family of the left" all singing from the same songbook—the rivals on the left knew exactly how to use shared concepts to compete fiercely with each other for hegemony within the broader left. Subsequently it became a matter of life and death for social democrats—a term that really attained its present meaning only in the 1950s—to put as much distance as they possibly could between themselves and the Communists. Nowadays, historians routinely read back into the 1910s and 1930s assumptions about the gulf between "social democrats" and "Marxists," assumptions that ride roughshod over much historical evidence.

Each of the major formations had its moment, a time when it seemed to articulate the deep-seated contradictions of the system and the means to overcome them. Each claimed to have fully absorbed and transcended the achievements of its predecessors. Indeed, many formations claimed exactly the same ancestors as their predecessors. Declaring its rivals so many dead letters, a formation striving for hegemony would still take care to borrow judiciously from them. The elements of "one socialism" were thus radically repositioned within the ensemble of another. The members of a new cohort in that way might take themselves to be connecting with a continuous tradition, even though in the very attempt to reconnect themselves to it they were changing the very tradition they wanted to see as unchanging.

Although we can puzzle out a pattern of cohorts and formations, then, we always have to be open to the possibility of surprise and the inevitability of debate. In various forms, some obviously vestigial and others more dynamic, all the major left formations developed in the Canadian political ecology survive to this day. One can still join a Socialist Party of Canada claiming descent from the party that was most significant in the period 1904–11, or a Communist Party of Canada whose heyday of general significance was 1921–37. Cohorts do take up a given set of ideas and practices at a given moment, but the formation they construct, if it is successful, will persist as an influence—albeit a waning one—long after the two and a half decades normally assigned them.

In the spirit of the many manifestos of the Canadian left—which somebody should anthologize in the future—I can summarize this "formations approach" in the form of a five-point program.

1. Capitalism, a socio-economic formation with real and material properties, which has predominantly been understood in modern Canada through the categories of liberal order, generates problems and contradictions that provide an opening for left (and in this context, down to our own period, "socialist") challenges. Nonetheless, these challenges do not emerge spontaneously from the soil of working-class (or other) struggles.

2. Structure-shifting "matrix-events" spark sudden and drastic moments of rebellion. Many people suddenly find it imperative to refuse the social world around them. It may end there, if there is no organized political formation to channel this refusal into more lasting shape. But if there is opportunity, refusal can lead to supersedure: the sense not only that the immediate oppression should be resisted, but also that the

entire structure making it possible should be contested. And supersedure—that collective moment of understanding that the suffering of today emerges from underlying contradictions in the social and economic structure—in turn can lead to systematization, the energetic collective pursuit of models and narratives that will make sense of, and preserve, this moment.

3. The applied sociology, historical analysis, and cultural networks developed by such leftists, although shaped by the orientation of each given group, are also used as ways of articulating their interests with those of much wider groups of people. They share a common language, identify common enemies, and anticipate a common future; and precisely to that extent, they constitute a formation. As a formation coheres, it becomes more and more capable of addressing a wide array of phenomena using coherent conceptual frameworks. The concepts at the heart of a left formation represent a significant symbolic and material investment. They are often adopted by a cohort drawn from a particular generation. Their development confronts other leftists with the dilemma of either identifying with or resisting them. Unlike a "paradigm" as conceptually developed within the philosophy of science, the "leftism" championed by a formation is not a system of concepts distinct from its rivals. When there is an out-and-out struggle for hegemony on the left—say, in the course of the Communist attempt to displace evolutionary socialists in the 1920s—there is not so much an exchange of insights as attempts to reduce and absorb one dialect by another. One leftism seeks not reconciliation with, but the absorption of, the other leftism. But such patterns, somewhat reminiscent of "paradigmatic

struggles" in science and often bitterly fought out in the open, may conceal how much all the significant parties and forces borrow and cross-reference each other within any given period.

4. Leftism reaches a certain "fixity" in formal institutions, manifestos, position papers, and so on, all of which are useful for the historian as ways of exploring the lived experiences of a given cohort. Yet these institutions and documents can also be quite misleading. We are tempted to read the manifesto transparently, at "face value" (and forget its implicit message), or to take the party at its word (and forget its limited life span and, possibly, limited counter-hegemonic commitment). Parties and their declarations are of primary interest for what they tell us about the socialist formations that are their conditions of possibility. They are features of the landscape, but reconnaissance uses them as clues to the tectonic plates underneath. Socialism happens when these people willingly throw themselves into the revolutionary dialectic of the historical process, themselves becoming one element of a contradiction whose resolution cannot be foreseen in advance.

This interpretation no longer focuses on the formal parties and the leading individuals as *the* core of the history of Canadian left. The parties are significant, as are their leaders, but the significance lies in their existence as the vehicles of attempts to think and live otherwise, to understand and escape the contradictions of bourgeois order. They are moments of a more profound process, which they grasp only partially and temporarily. Through attempting to develop the contradictions of liberal order, they illuminate its central features. And in this sense, one that looks at each leftism as a kind of experiment in living otherwise, the question of "success or failure" is posed very differently than in a conventional reading. A party or group might stand as a significant "success" even if it elects no members to any legislature and leads no great strikes, if its words and deeds nonetheless can be shown to have compelled change within the system.

5. An inclusive narrative of a given moment of Canadian socialism can be written in terms of the major figures, parties, currents, texts, and debates. The logic of transition to the "next moment" lies in the (implicit and explicit) contradictions inherent in any socialist network; and especially in the gap between the post-liberal socialist ideal and the contingencies of survival in a liberal order. Each formation can be identified not only in terms of its way with words but also by the core political contradictions built into it. A full history of Canadian socialism would thus trace both the continuities between one moment and the next, and the gaps and overlaps between formations. It would pay special attention to linguistic innovations and to symptomatic silences, the moments when the formation has seemingly "sealed" a contradictory reality within its own terms, and those when the "seal" is broken.

These points lay out a model-building agenda. But historical reality is always more complicated and wayward than the interpretive schemas brought to interpret it, necessary as they doubtless are. Because liberal order has persisted, attaining in Canada a status unusual in world terms, its enduring cultural power has been enormous. In Canada the left's moments of supersedure have always been followed by decades-long wars of position, through which the leading left formation is absorbed by a liberal passive revolution that seeks to liquidate its militant adversaries. For many, leftism is sentimentally consigned to the realm of youthful simplicities. Having a real life with a real job means the swift or gradual erasure of even the memory of thinking that there could be an otherwise. For others, the moment of supersedure must be defended at all costs against compromise with the liberal order. What one person tries to forget or smiles at indulgently as youthful enthusiasm, the other dogmatically defends against all critics. In the latter case, the past assumes an ever more vivid reality, the truth takes on an ever more solid certainty, and the enemies on the inside, on the left, come to be as permanently demarcated as any of the political enemies outside.

Rather than either sentimentality or sectarianism, a more politically useful and intellectually interesting approach would be a much more inclusive narrative—written in terms of major and minor figures, parties, currents, texts, and debates—that seeks to track leftist formations in all their complex diversity. This would be a kind of left history that makes it possible to imagine a tradition that is both discontinuous and continuous: discontinuous in that it focuses on the "breaks" and "differences in focus" that separate one formation from another; continuous in that it nonetheless makes it possible to theorize a Canadian left as the pursuit of a path out of the labyrinth of a persisting liberal order.

FIVE

Mapping the Canadian Movement

ALTHOUGH THE Canadian left as a continuous, post-liberal, formation-generating force can be dated back only to the 1890s, anticipations of socialism can be found much earlier. Indeed, left ideas and activism in Canada go back more than 180 years—to at least 1829, when the ideas of Scottish mill-owner Robert Owen formed the basis of a colony established in Bright's Grove, near Sarnia, Ontario. In New Lanark, Scotland, Owen had become the prophet of a new world, in a message delivered from the strife-ridden landscape of the Industrial Revolution. He pitched his model communities and philanthropic schemes to anyone who would listen. In North America, where Owen himself could be found promoting co-operative communities between 1824 and 1829, the Owenites fit within much broader patterns of "communist" community-building. In Canada, as it turned out, one Henry Jones (1776–1852), who had retired on half-pay from the Royal Navy, was converted by Owen's schemes for villages of "unity and co-operation," and Bright's Grove was his project. The builders of the short-lived colony named Maxwell that Jones planted near Sarnia may well have been the first people in North America to call themselves "socialists."[1] That said, the experiment at Bright's Grove was too exceptional, short-lived, and enigmatic to have exercised much lasting influence, even as a memory, on the Canadian left.

Much later, in 1900, Finnish socialists under the leadership of Matti Kurikka, a prominent Social Democrat and philosopher, established a utopian socialist community at Sointula on Malcolm Island, British Columbia. The project may have attracted as many as two thousand people before it collapsed in 1904, partly because of disputes over free love—classically a difficult issue in intentional utopian communities—and, probably more crucially, because of Sointula's location, which did not allow for agricultural self-sufficiency but did require commercial ties with the burgeoning capitalist economy of the lower B.C. mainland.[2]

Maxwell and Sointula did not become models for more influential movements. In contrast to the United States, where there were scores of utopian experiments in the nineteenth century, with an impact that lasted well into the twentieth, there would be no lasting "utopian formation" in Canada—and therein may rest a little-explored but historically significant difference between the divergent lefts of these two North American countries. In general U.S. socialism, in its many formations, often speaks in an apocalyptic "high diction" of cities upon the hill and saving all of humanity. Canadian socialism has always been significantly less inspiring in rhetoric and yet more durable as a pragmatic adaptation to a specific political order.

From these early beginnings until the present time, though, we can trace five major left formations in

Canada, all of them forms of "socialism"—and with a sixth post-socialist left formation under construction today. In the earliest formation, 1890–1919, socialism was defined as the applied science of social evolution. Then, in a second formation, 1917–39, it became tightly defined as revolutionary seizure of power by a working class under the leadership of a vanguard party. In the long period of 1935 to 1970, representing a third formation, socialism was once again redefined, this time as a movement aiming at national economic and social management executed by a bureaucratic planning state answerable to parliament. A fourth left formation, 1965–80, saw socialism defined as the overcoming of individual and national alienation through grassroots liberation movements; and a fifth formation, 1967–90, focused closely on the liberation of women from the domination of men. Finally, in the formation emerging today, leftism consists of Canadian participation in a global justice movement that resists the planetary hegemony of capitalism and argues for locally controlled societies and economies consistent with the survival of humanity on Earth.

THE SOCIAL EVOLUTIONARIES

In nineteenth-century Canada "Marx" was set to work only episodically. As early as the 1870s, an extract from *Capital* was published in a prominent, and otherwise quite conservative, Ontario working-class newspaper. In the 1880s, at least one Halifax employer worried, rather melodramatically, about the prospects of "communism" gaining influence among local longshoremen. Left labour-reform sentiments can be found in the Provincial Workmen's Association, a general union that flourished from 1879 to 1908, principally among coal-mine workers in Nova Scotia, and the Knights of Labor, whose influence, concentrated in Ontario and Quebec, was marked in the 1880s.[3]

The first free-standing newspaper that was primarily socialist in content was the Toronto *Labor Advocate*, published from 1890 to 1891. In 1887, with the assistance of the renowned U.S. political economist Henry George, who had become his friend and mentor, its editor Phillips Thompson brought out *The Politics of Labor*, an eloquent defence of a working-class democracy. *The Politics of Labor*, published in the United States, was at base a long description of Thompson's own moment of supersedure as he came to grips with the corruption and class bias of U.S. politics. Significantly, this pioneering book for the Canadian left drew extensively upon the ideas of the British philosopher and sociologist Herbert Spencer—whose concept of social evolution was almost endlessly cited to support the left in the years before 1920—to make its critique of U.S. politics and society. Thompson was developing a radical-democratic approach to extend counter-hegemonic ideas beyond a narrow base in the industrial working class (a small minority in this period) to encompass producers as a whole. For all their differences, many farmers and workers could agree on the moral bankruptcy and irrationality of the party system. If they could ally on little else, they could find agreement in the idea of a democratic revolution, exemplified in Canada by the demand that MPs be subject to recall, that referenda be held on popular issues, and that legislation be directly initiated in the rank and file.

Thompson believed that the freedoms formally guaranteed by a liberal order could become real forces in daily life only if they were taken up as causes by a large working-class movement. What had once been unrealistic and utopian could now, thanks especially to the forces of social evolution that Spencer had so brilliantly analyzed, be brought within grasp. Thompson suggestively drew attention to the absence of a theoretical vocabulary that could be used to capture the idea that the few had monopolized the Earth's resources and forced the many to compete with each other for the means of livelihood. "There is no word in the language which will answer," he exclaimed. Like Duncan's murder in *Macbeth*, the "social crime" that condemned so many to poverty was "a deed without a name." Soon he would find that word—capitalism—as well as the word for capitalism's transcendence in a realm of freedom: socialism.

In this period, to become a socialist in North America often meant agreement with the ideas of Edward Bellamy, developed in his phenomenally successful novel *Looking Backwards*, which describes in great detail a highly rational, post-capitalist "realm of freedom." Thompson announced his conversion to the socialism of Bellamy in December 1890. He then went on to become chairman of the Municipal Committee of the Bellamyite Toronto Nationalist Club, which became active in 1891. (It must stand as one of the nicer ironies of Canadian left history that the first of many "socialist nationalists" in the country were the boundary-blind apostles of a U.S. radical.)

In the *Labor Advocate*, Thompson, once the defender of orthodox liberal political economy, now used the language of the new theory. "Capitalism," he argued, "is the power by which labor is robbed of the greater portion of its earnings."[4] This choice of words indicated a transition in his perspective. Throughout *The Politics of Labor* and his earlier journalism, there was an assumption that capital and labour might fairly and democratically arbitrate their differences; but from his conversion in 1890 on, the *Labor Advocate* argued for the essential and irreconcilable conflict between the interests of capitalists and wage-workers. The wealth of the former was squeezed from the labour of the latter.

The political economist Henry George provided many of this cohort with their first experience of a radical step-by-step critical evaluation of the capitalist system. Spencer's social-evolutionary theories, which to a considerable extent underpinned George's work, spoke as powerfully as those of Marx to anyone who wanted to systematize this insight into a body of thought and practice. So too did the anthropological writings of Lewis Henry Morgan, who constructed an interpretation of the social evolution of Amerindian societies that was to deeply influence Frederick Engels. The U.S.-based Socialist Labor Party (SLP) established the first general network of socialist organizations in Canada, ran the first socialist candidates at the municipal and provincial levels in Ontario, and even in 1901 adopted a Canadian constitution. Daniel De Leon, the SLP's brilliant if abrasive leader, exerted an intellectual influence in Canada that was more widespread than the size of his party would suggest. The SLP would long remain a vigorous voice for an approach to a scientific-evolutionary leftism that combined Morgan, Engels, and Marx.[5]

The first homegrown socialist movement with dominion-wide ambitions was the Canadian Socialist League (CSL), enthusiasm for which ignited, almost simultaneously in Montreal and Toronto, in the summer of 1899. Its Toronto organizing convention in November 1901, although ostensibly aimed at creating an Ontario Socialist League limited to the province, marked the first solid attempt to launch a pan-Canadian socialist organization. Within two years Marxist materialists and Protestant ministers were at loggerheads in a struggle within the organization. In British Columbia the United Socialist Labor Party emerged in April 1900 as a breakaway from the SLP. In October 1900 British Columbia held its first socialist convention, with a red flag flying proudly over a local meeting hall. In 1901 the Socialist Party of British Columbia emerged as a counterpart to the Socialist Party of America. In autumn 1902 James Hawthornthwaite, elected to the provincial legislature on an independent labour platform in Nanaimo, in the centre of the coal-mining district, joined the short-lived Revolutionary Socialist Party of Canada.

By 1904, following complex mergers and splits with local labour parties and an affiliation with many from the CSL, the Socialist Party of Canada (SPC) had emerged in British Columbia as the first electorally significant socialist party in Canada. The SPC became renowned for its vigorous denunciations of the "palliatives" that less radical leftists might prescribe for the ills of capitalism, its advocacy of a "single-plank" platform that called for the revolutionary overthrow of the capitalist system, and its proud disavowal of any connection to the Second International—most of the socialist parties of Western Europe were affiliated to this body, which the SPC disparaged because it contained parties that were insufficiently revolutionary. Yet the SPC did nonetheless consider itself tied to the international socialist movement and admitted members of other European socialist parties who carried "clear cards" testifying to their legitimate membership in a European party. SPCers would be elected to provincial legislatures in British Columbia, Alberta, and Manitoba, but the party failed to elect a single federal MP.[6]

The early years of the twentieth century also saw the emergence of a variety of local labour parties, many of them looking to the Independent Labour Party in Britain for inspiration. From 1907 on, those dissatisfied with the SPC's "single-plank" platform of socialist revolution attempted to create bodies more closely attached to the Second International. Many of these "diaspora socialists" were drawn from ethnic minorities, especially from the highly repressive Russian Empire. After 1911 they could rally to the Social Democratic Party of Canada (SDPC), which, in contrast to the SPC, allowed the minority language groups such ample scope for self-determination that they were rather more prominent, at least to the increasingly anxious police authorities, than was the overarching party to which they were affiliated.

In 1917 the Trades and Labour Congress of Canada, the country's largest labour federation, passed a resolution calling for the formation of "a political party which would unite the trade unions with the local socialist and labour parties in the provinces, and eventually become a national party"—although the Labour Party that resulted, a loose federation of provincial labour parties without much of a developed central structure, never quite lived up to this expectation. Nonetheless, the Federated Labour Party in British Columbia and the Independent Labour Party in Manitoba were major vehicles for political resistance in the 1920s.

To sum up this first formation, we can distil its socialism by providing answers to a number of salient questions.

- What is the purpose of left-wing activity? It is to hasten the processes of social evolution, which work similarly in nature and in society, and thereby to end the exploitation of labour by capital that explains the grievous suffering and glaring contradictions of an illogical and immoral system—such as the emergence of trusts, the proliferation of sweatshops, and the immiseration of labour.
- What, then, is socialism? It is the application of laws of social evolution, which—whether we consult them in the New Testament, Spencer's *First Principles*, or Marx's *Capital*—demonstrate that society is an evolving social organism. Arising from a moment of refusal of the most glaring aspects of the tyranny of capital in the age of the robber barons and monopolists, socialism takes an initial intuition into how much more interconnected human beings had become, and systematizes it into something that draws, heavily, upon social evolutionary theory, in particular the sociology of Herbert Spencer. Marx's theories—of surplus value, historical materialism, and class struggle—are all seen as specific applications of this more general theory of social evolution.

- Who are the most important agents in struggling for socialism? Workers—especially those who have mastered the science of social evolution and have grasped that they have it within their power, by electing socialists and preaching the gospel of socialism in public spaces, to disseminate the new knowledge to the public.
- What are the political structures of the formation? Apart from labour parties—until the postwar period, generally ad hoc organizations formed to contest specific elections—there are small propaganda organizations, which impose (explicitly or implicitly) rigorous standards for anyone who wants to be considered a real socialist, that is, a person who has mastered the science of social evolution. First formation parties do not define success or failure by election victories, and the role of a socialist parliamentarian is not primarily to introduce legislation but to use the legislature as a giant soapbox for socialist education. The classic parties of the first wave—SLP, CSL, SPC, and SDPC—are significant as educators, but not more so than other important bodies, including ethnic associations such as the Finnish Socialist Organization of Canada, which established halls wherein socialist education and community events could be combined. None of these groups are "parliamentary socialist parties" in a sense recognizable today. They are far more oriented to public propaganda, rabble-rousing, and education.
- What are the major characteristics that distinguish this formation from others? One peculiarity of the first formation is its emphasis on the scientific enlightenment of the people. It initiated a major debate over religion, fought out intensively between those who saw Christ as the exemplary socialist (including many of

the much-discussed advocates of the Social Gospel) and those who identified the entire Christian tradition as an ancient web of superstition (the less-famous but then-notorious advocates of atheism, "Free Thought," and other forms of heterodoxy). Many people fell in between the two. Sharply critical of the institutional church, they sought forms of religious expression that spoke directly to working-class struggles.

BOLSHEVIKS AND WORLD REVOLUTION

"Revolution" is the keyword of the second, largely Communist, formation that took shape after 1917. From 1917 to 1922 a massive labour revolt shook the Dominion. The Winnipeg General Strike in 1919 stands as its most famous single event, and the 1921 election of two left-wing labour members, J.S. Woodsworth and William Irvine, to the House of Commons was one of the more significant of its consequences.[7] The Communist Party of Canada was undoubtedly the most important single force within this formation, carrying a significance that today is often forgotten. Founded on 23 May 1921 at a secret convention in a barn near Guelph, Ontario, with sixteen people present—and at least one of them an RCMP agent who thoughtfully left behind a detailed summary of the discussion—it performed through most of the period 1917–37 a political and cultural role radically different from that of earlier propaganda parties. Yet it competed for hegemony with many other organizations and forces, and it shared its vocabulary of revolutionary change with others still.

The Industrial Workers of the World (IWW) anticipated the revolutionary wave in pre-war British Columbia and competed intensively with the CPC for hegemony within the revolutionary movement in Northern Ontario in the 1930s. The One Big Union, which for a decade made a sustained attempt to dislodge North American business unionism and to build a revolutionary labour movement that anticipated the radical democracy of living otherwise, was also a competitor with the CPC. The rivalry was sharpened by the Communist Party's pursuit of a policy (shaped in accordance with Lenin's advice) of entering mainstream labour organizations.[8]

Nonetheless, the foundation of the Communist Party of Canada undoubtedly gave shape and direction to a revolutionary "left turn" evident even before the Russian Revolution in 1917. Thanks in large part to the prestige of that revolution, to its powerful attraction for particular ethnic groups (Finns, Ukrainians, and Jews most prominently), and to the organizational discipline it inspired in its devotees, the Communist Party exerted an influence well beyond its limited numbers.

The CPC could claim to be the Canadian party representing the revolutionary strategy that had brought the Bolsheviks to power in Russia. It sidelined many competing radical organizations. In 1922 it set up a Workers' Party of Canada to be the above-ground voice of the Bolshevik persuasion in Canada, although—given that the Canadian climate did not really require an underground party—this pretense was gradually dropped. By 1925 the CPC was operating publicly under its own name, taking an active part in the Communist International (Comintern), the body set up to oversee member parties in their struggles to overthrow capitalism worldwide, and involving itself—although somewhat unwillingly, and mainly at the leadership level—in the debates pitting Leon Trotsky against Joseph Stalin after Lenin's death. (The CPC was one of the last in the world to take Stalin's side.) Communists were highly active in the 1920s, at a time when much of the labour movement was demoralized after the defeat of the massive labour revolt. In the 1930s, through the Workers' Unity League, Communists struggled to organize those workers whom other unions would not organize. They encountered vigorous resistance from the state, in the form of Section 98 of the Criminal Code of Canada, which allowed the RCMP to arrest those suspected of being Communists even if they had joined when the Party was not illegal.

After a serious schism in 1928 over the character of the Soviet Union and its leadership, the Party came under the leadership of Tim Buck, who would stay at its helm until 1961 and remain as its father figure until his death in 1973. Arrested with seven comrades in 1932 under Section 98, Buck was sentenced to Kingston Penitentiary; an attempt was evidently made to shoot him during a riot in the institution. He was released in 1934 to popular acclaim; such was the Party's popularity in Toronto that it could fill Maple Leaf Gardens to celebrate his release.

A major shift in the orientation of the Party occurred in 1935, when the Communist International decided to drop its harsh critique of social democrats as "social fascists" and opted instead to build alliances with them (and other parties)—a strategy generally called the Popular Front—to achieve such general objectives as support for the Republicans in the Spanish Civil War. Loyally backing the Soviet Union through the show trials of prominent Bolsheviks in 1937 and 1938, and in the Hitler-Stalin Pact of 1939, the party found itself once more on the defensive in the first two years of the Second World War. When it regained some of its influence in the period 1941–48, it would do so as a party with a new name and a radically different strategy.[9]

Reaching about sixteen thousand official members at its height (and several times that many people in related organizations), the Communists built the first large-scale party of the left in Canada. (The Canadian Labour Party, backed by the Trades and Labor Congress, was an episodic spectre by comparison; moreover, at times members of the CPC controlled it.) In certain significant quarters—among the Jews of Winnipeg, Toronto, and Montreal; the Finns of Northern Ontario; the Ukrainians of Western Canada—the CPC would provide thousands of leftists with their major, sustained experience of a left party. Associated with the Party were such groups as the Canadian Labor Defence League, the Women's Labor Leagues, the Young Communist League, the Workers' Sports League, and the Progressive Farmers' Educational League. Unions associated with the Workers' Unity League fought some of the most dramatic strikes of the early Depression. Alongside all of this official Communism was the phenomenon of dissident communism, to which Canada contributed many highly intelligent and dynamic activists and thinkers. Following a traumatic split in 1928, the brilliant Maurice Spector devoted his next twelve years to the struggle to refound the Communist movement, in ways that would remain faithful to the democratic revolutionary heritage that he identified with Bolshevism and that he believed was being betrayed by Stalin. Trotskyists and Stalinists, divided on many specific questions, nonetheless agreed that the Bolshevik Revolution served as the template for revolutionary activism in the West.[10]

What for the first formation was a direct relationship between the evolution of the cosmos and the ultimate victory of the cause was transformed by second-wave socialists into a relationship mediated by revolutionary activism. Revolutionary acts could accelerate the pace of history; in their absence the course of history could be set back. This was the reason for the formation's unflinching support for the Soviet Union. The basic, defining difference that separated the two formations was the new conception of the party. No longer primarily an instrument of propagandizing the truth, in a sense the Party now *was* that truth—the tangible demonstration of the power of Marx's revolutionary science. Through the Party, and by supporting the world's first workers' state, the adherents could blast through the prison-house of evolution and grasp a genuine realm of human freedom, in acts of revolutionary agency that fused the "abstract" analyses of Marx with the passionate rejection of a capitalist order. In the Communist formation the party form attained a new status as the central revolutionary agent that had only been hinted at in its earlier incarnation as a general socialist educator.

The Communist conceptual system had other distinctive attributes. Like the first formation, it spoke positively of "revolution," although in a Communist formation dedicated to defending and extending a real-world revolutionary state the term functioned in a different way. To be a Communist was to enlist in the world army of the revolution. It was not to imagine a distant inevitability. It was to fight for an immediate reality. The revolution had ceased to be a "myth," a man like Spector would say, and had become the "inspiring reality of a proletarian state." As well, evolution as the guarantor of socialism and truth was sidelined by the Party, which emerged as the "collective scientist" equipped to discern the true interests of the working class for which it spoke. There were new ways of ascertaining the truth. The somewhat general prognostications of the first wave were replaced with analyses that attempted to read the historical process with a precision that allowed for successful revolutionary intervention. There was a greatly heightened sense of *realpolitik* and the necessary costs of socialist politics. The new formation implied a much tighter relationship between theory and practice, an intensified sense that socialism was not just an aspect of evolution but also (to remind ourselves of Gramsci's discussion of "utopianism") an *objective possibility* that revolutionaries had to use, and use skilfully, in the pressing circumstances of the present day.

This was decidedly not a formation for well-meaning amateurs but for professional revolutionaries. Rather paradoxically, this was also a formation that involved, for that very reason, a heightened awareness that all political action took place in a context and might have unanticipated consequences. Many writings of the time show a new certainty that a correct line could connect the present with the future—the party as "collective midwife" might "actively manage" socialism's birth (but, conversely, through its "adventurism" or "opportunism," it could also engineer a miscarriage). Finding and adhering to this correct line formed an urgent business. Failure to do so was not a forgivable human failing but a crime against the revolution.

Another distinction of the second formation was that it put the question of class to different work. Both of the first two formations formally defined class in terms of a relationship to the means of production, but in the first formation the members of the "working class" were often presented as the credulous, none-too-swift consumers of capitalistic pabulum. In the second formation the "proletariat" was the working class that within itself, and if properly led by a disciplined leadership, had the wherewithal to rapidly overthrow the bourgeoisie. The working-class dupes of the first formation became the proletarian heroes of the second, although the bulk of them still tended to be seen as culturally and politically backward vessels. Proletarian struggle came to be conceived as the vital—at times the only—consideration for those who wanted to subvert the system. Objective analysis would illuminate not just the trends of social evolution over the very long term—the "cosmic" frame often preferred by the first formation—but also allow enthusiasts to grasp the "micro" analysis of the immediate political situation. It was possible for true Communists to define the interests of workers quite apart from the workers' own experience.

The theses put forward by Lenin, with their adamant insistence on the subordination of the various national parties to the Communist International and of the members of the Party to the central committee, were not ones on which a middle ground could easily be found. "Vanguardism," the combined tactics of democratic centralism within and united front without, and the emphasis on revolutionary direct action, both before and after the inauguration of the dictatorship of the proletariat—on these and other issues any search for a bland consensus, whether at the time or in the subsequent history books, was doomed.

Probably at no time—although there is contrary evidence from 1932 to 1938, when the CPC made truly amazing gains in influence through the Canadian Labor Defence League—did the majority of Canadian leftists embrace Leninism. Most Canadian leftists would have identified more readily with labour parties, the emergent CCF, and such struggling industrial union organizations as the One Big Union, the All-Canadian Congress of Labour, and even the Industrial Workers of the World (which enjoyed a resurgence in this period not common in the rest of North America). Yet each and every one of these non-Leninist bodies had to deal with an energetic, disciplined, and fearless Communist presence. Leftists throughout this period can be heard wrestling actively with Communist arguments and, revealingly, even publishing in the Communist press.

It would thus be a serious error, both theoretically and politically, to minimize the role of the CPC. The first large-scale party of Canadian socialism taught socialists in general how to organize a party. It enjoyed striking support among Jews, Finns, and Ukrainians. Those who passed through the CPC—and as elsewhere over the decades the ranks of the ex-Communists grew exponentially, as each one of the Party's line-changes exacted its psychological and cultural price, most obviously in 1956—did not forget all that they had learned about party discipline and structure. In this tendency the Canadian experience is probably somewhat unusual. Elsewhere the Communists emerged in a left context already deeply colonized by electorally minded social-democratic parties. In Canada, as Spector insistently pointed out in his strategic writings of this period, the Communists functioned through much of the 1920s and early 1930s in a left that lacked any authoritative social-democratic alternative. In some places, like Spadina in Toronto and North-End Winnipeg, the CPC became the leading left party.

To sum up the second formation, we can—as we did with its predecessor—distil its approach by asking a number of pertinent questions.

- What is the purpose of left-wing activity? In this case it is to overthrow the capitalist state and replace it with a dictatorship of the proletariat, which will over time achieve a genuine people's democracy by the liquidation of capitalist relations of production, distribution, and exchange.
- What, then, is socialism? It is the rule of the industrial working class, guided by a vanguard party made up of professional revolutionaries trained in the science of Marxism-Leninism. More specifically, being a socialist meant being fully engaged in the class struggle as defined and strategized by the Party. This was the core socialist position.
- Who are the most important agents in struggling for socialism? The proletarian party and the working class—the first guiding the second. The Party works through a myriad of different groups, sometimes

overtly and sometimes otherwise, but with a single purpose—that of overthrowing the established political order.

- What are the political structures of the formation? The vanguard party—ideally made up of the advanced workers, and representative of the cultural makeup of the country (but in practice heavily concentrated among immigrant working-class communities in Toronto, Montreal, the Lakehead, Winnipeg, and Vancouver). This party is in turn integrated into the Comintern, whose instructions it is supposed to carry out (how faithfully and in what detail would depend on circumstances). A further form is the active insertion of the Party into the trade union movement.
- What are the major characteristics that distinguish this formation from others? One peculiarity of the second formation is its paradoxical combination of marked localism—the CPC was always rather more a federation of ethnic radicals than a strictly "Bolshevized" party, even if in theory it struggled mightily against this demographic reality—and an equally pronounced reliance on the international Communist movement, centred in the Communist International in Moscow. (Brutally victimized by Stalin's purges, the Communist International was, some years before its formal abolition by Stalin in the 1940s, no longer the active shaping force it had once been for the world Communist movement.) To an extent not experienced in any other formation, socialists within this one are not only shaped by both the benefits and the drawbacks of affiliation with a massive international movement, with enormous resources at its disposal, but also often increasingly driven by political and cultural

imperatives strikingly removed from political cultures shaped by the Enlightenment.

Reconnaissance can, perhaps, provide a new way of writing about the forever controversial Communist moment, in which a variety of writers have made a heavy investment. For some of the emergent state-planning social democrats, the CPC became entirely a figure of loathing—a hostility sharpened by the extreme electoral damage that any association with Communists would entail for them in most political settings in Canada. For dissident Communists, the tone struck in discussing the CPC is even sharper—for them, it is the party that betrayed Lenin's world revolution and was implicated in the murder of Trotsky. For many postwar immigrants from the Communist regimes of Eastern Europe, "actually existing socialism" in the East bloc was associated with double-think, murderous intrigues, and the obliteration of democracy. From the 1960s to the 1980s, revelations of mass murder in the gulag cast a dark shadow over those who had apologized for Stalin from the 1930s to the 1950s. The recent release of archival materials from the time of the Great Terror has intensified, not mitigated, the sense of a Soviet descent into a living hell. This, for many, is all that can now be said about the second formation.[11]

For others, the moment of the CPC nonetheless has many positive qualities. Studies of left culture in the 1930s note the extent to which the Party inspired a host of experiments in theatre, writing, folk music, and the visual arts. Many labour historians have noted the role of CPCers in founding many of Canada's largest and most important industrial unions. In many of these organizations, such as the Canadian Seamen's Union, the CPC seems to have played a constructive and responsible role, nurturing rank-and-file democracy and effectively fighting for the seamen's interests. Many memoirists have recalled the warm community atmosphere of the CPC cultural institutions, such as the ethnic choirs and summer camps. Others have highlighted the innovative role of CPC writers in such fields as history and political economy. For people such as these, the CPC—despite its readily conceded limitations—played an essentially positive role in bringing a more rigorous and systematic Marxist praxis to Canadians.

A reconnaissance will not resolve this schism—it is most likely irresolvable—but it will try to see the CPC from a different angle. It would look at the Communist formation, as it did its predecessor, as an experiment in living otherwise, with both strengths and weaknesses as a challenge to liberal order. The formation's consolidation will look differently when it is seen not as some inexplicable eruption or the result of some inevitable unfolding of laws of history but as a result of a hegemonic struggle within the left, in which the first and second formations clashed over left strategy, tactics, and philosophy. From the standpoint of the second formation, the Russian Revolution imposed a stark "before-and-after" narrative on the history of the left. It separated the "real" from the "abstract," the "revolutionary" from the "armchair" socialists. The second formation oversimplified its antecedents by identifying them with a supposedly unified social-democratic tradition to which it was opposed.

Left somewhat undertheorized were such questions as the specific nature of the Canadian economy and the role of the Canadian state within it. Certainly the waning influence of the formation after 1937 merits careful scrutiny. In essence, the international Communist movement changed its political strategy in 1935, when it adopted the policy of the Popular Front. The notion of building a multiparty democratic front was a dramatic line-change for a party that, one year before, had brought out a major publication denouncing the CCF as an agent of fascism. Over the roughly quarter-century that Communists formed a very important part of the Canadian left—from 1921 to 1946 or so—how did they manage their relationship with the broader left? In the transition from the workplace-focused vanguardist Third Period to the nation-focused Popular Front, how consciously did the Party change its conception of historical agency? In the application of "universal" Communist International criteria and debates to the Canadian situation, did CPC language suggest a gradual indigenization?

Here the extraordinary significance of the CPC's presentation to the Rowell-Sirois Commission on Federal-Provincial Relations stands out: a book-length document that laid out the Party's attempt to systematically interpret (and apply) a reading of Canadian history. Another key is the pioneering Marxist historical work of Stanley Ryerson, who—building on discussions of the national question in the international movement—developed the first substantial left theorization of the national question in Quebec. The more recent opening of millions of files of Communist International documents now raises the possibility of debates that leave the old positions behind.

There is also an enormous opportunity for developing a comparative history of Communist parties in the North Atlantic world—an exercise that might elicit practical lessons into ways of living otherwise. For example, what were the gains and losses of the policy of focusing so intensively on the working-class movement, in a country in which (by most Marxist definitions) the industrial working class was in the minority? Did Communist thought in Canada generally lack empirical and logical tests for its propositions—thereby resembling what some have called it, a "secular religion"? Or do the documents reveal a capacity to adjust tactical and strategic means to clearly articulated ends?

Then too, what was the exact chain of events that led to the destruction of the Communist Labor Progressive Party as a serious federal electoral challenge in 1945, when Igor Gouzenko, a clerk in the Soviet embassy in Ottawa, announced the existence of a "spy ring" and brought down the Party's one sitting MP, Fred Rose of Montreal? Did the Party have any room to manoeuvre, or did it even fully comprehend the implications, of this fatal development? (After the Gouzenko debacle, the party's successes were largely confined to the provincial and municipal levels; but in places such as Toronto, Winnipeg, and Vancouver, and in the peace movement, it maintained a presence down to the 1970s.)

A careful analysis of these questions in their specific contexts could lead to a much more analytical appraisal, more realistic than either celebratory or condemnatory, of the Bolshevik formation and more in keeping with the great international transformation now underway in the writing of the history of Western Communism.[12]

RADICAL PLANNERS AND STATE BUILDERS

In the mid-1930s a third, more clearly parliamentary formation emerged, related to but clearly distinguishable from the first two. (It is also not to be simply equated with the social democracy of the post-1960s NDP.) The Co-operative Commonwealth Federation displaced the CPC as the major party of the left in the decade following 1937—with both parties fighting each other on the terrain of the newly legitimized trade unions of the 1940s and a decade later in the highly charged atmosphere of the Cold War, battles that continue to subtly envenom much of the historical writing about them even today. It was a struggle that generated fine historical descriptions and figures in many general accounts of the "CCF-NDP tradition"—a term implicitly suggesting that there is one continuous national history linking the NDP of today with the CCF of the 1930s. There is much to be said for such a vertical approach—factually, many CCFers did become New Democrats in the 1960s, seeing in the new party simply a rejigging of the old. But there is also a case to be made that, ideologically and structurally, the leftism of the CCF can be clearly distinguished from the leftisms that came before and after.

The key to the third formation was what Eley has usefully called "Radical Planism."[13] Within the third formation, terms that had been secondary in earlier formations—"state," "nation," and "plan"—did different work than ever before. Others—"class struggle," "dictatorship of the proletariat," "wage slavery"—were sidelined. The question of transforming the existing Canadian state into a socialist state became the central question of politics. This was not the mild-mannered prescription that it might at first appear to be. Radical Planism entailed a more or less comprehensive socialization of much of the Canadian economy. It involved a dramatic rethinking of conventional parliamentary democracy, which was now to be supplemented with a much-strengthened "scientific" grasp of social and economic reality. Deploring the more dictatorial aspects of the Soviet Union, this tendency did express admiration for the achievements of its Five Year Plans and the egalitarianism of its thoroughly renovated social order.

"CCF" was the commonly used name for the Co-operative Commonwealth Federation: Farmer-Labour-Socialist. The full title is a richly suggestive echo of the first formation, within which the party was first formed and its leaders first educated. The early CCF included an assortment of socialist and other groups, many of them more oriented to the soapbox than the ballot box. In the initial conception these groupings were to be loosely joined together in a "federation." They were not to be melted into the "monolithic party" that the Bolsheviks thought was the only proper venue for a truly scientific socialism. In the 1920s its key figures were prairie stalwarts: J.S. Woodsworth, veteran of the Social Gospel movement within the Methodist Church and a participant in the Winnipeg General Strike, and William Irvine, an alumnus of the United Farmers of Alberta and the author of the immensely suggestive *The Farmers in Politics* and *Co-*

operative Government. In 1926 Woodsworth used his considerable moral authority and leadership to wrest old-age pensions from the wavering Liberal government of William Lyon Mackenzie King.[14]

In 1931 a group of six left-leaning members of parliament met on Parliament Hill to plan the formation of a new political organization, an alliance of various progressive and labour bodies. The Communists, the largest single party on the Canadian left, moved swiftly to denounce the emergent party, which they saw as reformist and naive, perhaps even actively fascist.

After 1935, in competition with the CPC, which in many respects, at least down to the late 1930s, was more than its equal in influence within the trade-union movement and in some areas electorally, the CCF gradually took on some of its competitor's attributes. Here the Marxist David Lewis, its brilliant new moving spirit, was of great influence. The task of writing the platform of the new party was delegated to the newly formed League for Social Reconstruction, a body founded in 1931–32, centred in Montreal and Toronto, and led by university intellectuals. Among its more eminent members were Frank Underhill, Eugene Forsey, King Gordon, and F.R. Scott. In such books as *Social Planning for Canada* (1935) and *Democracy Needs Socialism* (1938), the League put forward the case for Radical Planism. In some CCF documents, state ownership was the default position, whereas private ownership of the means of production, distribution, and exchange was defended only in special or unusual cases. Nationalize the banks. Extend co-operative institutions and make them the template of a new social order. Use the taxation system to achieve full social equality. End Canada's colonial status.

Communists derided such idealistic demands. Later the NDPers tried to present the CCF as a party simply keen on establishing compassionate social programs. Historians influenced by the New Left dined out for years on its many blind spots and middle-class illusions. The CCF's apologists and critics failed to recognize that the "Canada" the CCF was pushing for in the 1930s would have looked a lot like the planned state imagined by Edward Bellamy—an author, not coincidentally, whose writings were enthusiastically circulated within the party. This formation was not, actually, talking about a piecemeal process of reform at all. On the basis of this ultra-radical platform the party won 15.6 per cent of the popular vote and returned twenty-eight members to the House of Commons in 1945.

Perhaps the movement's most famous single statement was the Regina Manifesto, which was presented to the CCF's founding convention in 1933. This document, which came complete not only with a detailed moderate program for economic management but also with a clarion call at its conclusion for the end of capitalism, is conventionally remembered as a high point of Canadian radical thought. Something about it will always warm the souls of many Canadian leftists. Revealingly, no earlier manifesto from the movement resonated as strongly with succeeding generations. It combines the most soaring phrases of radicalism with the most pragmatic considerations of how life might be made better in the here and now. It may well be the only manifesto in the world socialist tradition that demands both the eradication of capitalism and the provision of railway level crossings.

It was a winning combination—prairie pragmatism combined with a dramatic sense that the world must be changed from top to bottom. With the formation of the country's first CCF provincial government in Saskatchewan in 1944, under the leadership of Baptist minister T.C. Douglas, the CCF clearly attained a new status. Like Maurice Spector in his completely different formation, CCFers could now proclaim that their socialism had moved from myth to reality. From 1944 to 1964 Saskatchewan would come to be regarded as a laboratory for an entirely new approach to the state in North America. Its Crown corporations, planning bodies, and most of all its medicare plan attracted national attention and, eventually in the latter case, national emulation.

At the same time the CCFers' Canada-wide experience of the 1950s was generally bleak, with the party being reduced from its twenty-eight seats in 1945 to only eight in 1958 (with a mere 9.5 per cent of the vote). In the climate of the Cold War, the party moderated its program, as evidenced in the 1956 Winnipeg Declaration of Principles, which—at least on one interpretation—represented a significant "liberalization" of the militant Radical Planism of the Regina Manifesto. In 1956 the Canadian Labour Congress saw fit to call on "liberally minded Canadians" to launch a new party, which would in time unite middle-class professionals with labour and farmers. The idea was that the new party would be roughly similar to the left-wing of the Democratic Party in the United States. In 1961, after many debates, the CCF was transformed into the

New Democratic Party at a convention in Ottawa, where it adopted a platform that might be termed "liberal leftist" rather than socialist. Yet many socialists persisted in the NDP. By 1965 many of its members were being radicalized as part of the struggle against the U.S. war in Vietnam, and some were rallying to New Left organizations.[15]

By conceptualizing the period from 1935 to 1965 as one of Radical Planism, dominated by a left formation committed to "national state management," we can take a fresh look at the CCF in a way that brings out its context, originality, and lasting contribution. It is striking that, although some important figures of the early CCF were "first formationists" in their thought—including Woodsworth and Irvine, both of them steeped in the language of Spencerian social organicism—the de facto driving force of the party after 1936 was a new cohort, typified by David Lewis, which articulated a political position quite close to that of the Independent Labour Party in Britain. Lewis's greatest single achievement on the left was probably the alliance he achieved with many elements of the labour movement—a tactic he justified in class terms.[16]

This new cohort was, to an extent now somewhat forgotten and that many CCFers would later deliberately try to obscure, strongly influenced by Marx. "There is no cheap solution of the problem of social reconstruction," proclaimed Eugene Forsey, one of its most prominent and influential intellectuals (and later a Liberal senator):

> There is no escaping the cross. The devil of social injustice goeth not out but by grappling with the

> fundamental issues. This generation seeketh after a sign, and there shall be no sign given it but the sign of the prophet Marx. Until Christians learn to understand and apply the lessons of Marxism they cannot enter into the Kingdom of Heaven—nor, probably, can any one else.[17]

It is no great stretch to see in F.R. Scott and David Lewis's *Make This Your Canada* (1943), the most popular left-wing publication of the 1940s, a performance of "Marx" adapted to a country that had recently put a good deal of its economy into public hands.[18] This tendency suggests the subterranean connections, never really explored with sufficient subtlety, between the second formation and the third. After the outbreak of the Cold War the CCF had everything to gain and nothing to lose by suggesting that it and the Communist Party had always been totally opposed to each other on the fundamental question of democracy. The convention even arose of referring to the "democratic left" as an entirely different species, radically distinguished from all the putatively "undemocratic" leftists who had gone before.

The conventional dichotomizing strategy pitting Communists against CCFers—the "revolutionaries" versus the "democratic left"—misses important questions that a more horizontal analysis opens up. In many respects the CPC—Canada's largest party of the left down to the late 1930s—instructed the CCF in the arts of party-building, political-economic analysis, and strategy. One of the most important lessons it taught the CCF was that a stable and powerful party had to be anchored in the working class—a linkage later achieved through the emergent labour bureaucracies. The CCF, which in many studies figures as the CPC's antithesis, incarnated, from 1936 to its demise in the 1960s, some of the attributes of the vanguard party, including a canon of official, must-read literature, a hierarchical top-down leadership structure, strict party discipline, and a tough line with minorities within the organization. A great deal of significance can be read into the transformation of the party in the mid-1930s, initiated by Woodsworth and carried much further by Lewis, away from the model of a loosely knit confederation of parties and movements to a more unified and centralized political machine.

The third formation marginalized—although at the local level it did not necessarily silence—an older language of class struggle shared by the first two formations. It set in its place a new language of national management and consolidation. This work had the effect not only of taking it into exciting new theoretical terrain—one more open to modern conceptions of politics and economics—but also of making the entire left highly vulnerable to an intensified liberal politics of passive revolution. Many historians underline the significance of the moment in the 1940s when Prime Minister Mackenzie King realized that the CCF was leading in the polls. Those within the formation believed that they might well be called upon to actually *govern*, and in Saskatchewan they were.

Value-free science and planning came to be esteemed as fundamental aspects of "modernity"—science could be organized for the people. Members of the first formation had believed that cosmic evolution underwrote socialist activism. The second formation had implicitly upheld a more dialectical conception of truth as that which emerged within the party as it engaged in revolutionary *praxis*. The third formation developed an emphasis that the truth was "out there," empirically accessible to (generally university-trained) social scientists and economists.

The third formation's Radical Planism owed much to the CPC, to the model of the Soviet Union—upheld in *Make This Your Canada* as an important model of a planning state, if unfortunately an undemocratic one—and to the general principle that professionals could arrive at value-free judgments. "Marx" was esteemed in this cohort, at least initially (after the onset of the Cold War, he would be cited much less frequently), but as an empirical social scientist, not a revolutionary sociologist or political theorist.

Just as there will probably never be a consensus on the Communists, so too—but for different reasons—will a happy convergence probably always elude conversations about the CCFers. Orthodox Marxists will always find them naive. They will cite the middle-class bias of their leadership, their waning interest in developing counter-hegemonic ideas, and their gradual absorption by the very liberal order that socialism by definition critiques. It also sticks in the Marxists' craw that the CCFers, in the Canadian left's most bitter civil war, beat the Reds for leadership of the labour movement and the left.

Orthodox New Democrats will probably always try to present the legacy of the CCF in nationalistic terms—the "party that changed Canada" and the "conscience of the country" martyring itself in the interests of the nation. Victimization would become a component of the stories that CCFers and later NDPers would tell themselves about their history. The CCF, they would say, was robbed of a fair chance at power by underhanded demagogic election campaigns—which, for example, wrenched quotations from *Make This Your Canada* and other radical publications, taking them out of context to make them appear much more revolutionary than they were. There is much truth in this; but there is also some naiveté.[19]

Hegemonic politics, to loosely paraphrase Chairman Mao, is not a dinner party. *Make This Your Canada* outlined, in ways that hundreds of thousands of Canadians evidently found convincing, a way of combining Marxian notions of a planned realm of freedom with parliamentary government and civil liberties. It anticipated a more or less comprehensive socialization of vast tracts of the Canadian economy. The wrath the book aroused in the business community was a predictable measure of the radicalism of its proposals. *Make This Your Canada* is the book to read if you want to see what a Canadian left formation might do with a *serious chance at power*—a real possibility of remaking political and cultural hegemony. It goes so far as to anticipate what Prime Minister M.J. Coldwell (the CCF leader) would say to the voters once he was elected—and one of the things he delivers is a warning to business leaders, phrased politely but forcibly, that "resistance is futile."

The book is a celebration of a specific kind of socialist state: one in which democracy is supplemented by comprehensive and systematic state planning. In place of the world-transforming "working class," now basically thought of more prosaically as a "labour movement" that should be guaranteed collective bargaining rights, the third formation thinks in terms of the "Canadian people." And in place of the marked internationalism of both the first and second formations, the third wrapped itself in the flag. The people could be as one, excepting those few speculators and monopolists whose future in the new Canada would be non-existent.

In its clearest articulation—*Make This Your Canada*—the third formation thus put forward a conception of its goal as the construction of a sleek, efficient, modernized, centrally planned state. In later liberal social-democratic accounts of the CCF, the party is treated as though it was simply about the introduction of social security programs. Actually, the idea of inflating partial welfare schemes into overall strategies for social change is *explicitly critiqued and rejected* in the text. The planning state envisaged by the CCF would be devoted to bringing full employment, continuous production, democratic participation of the people in the economy, an expanding national income, an "equitable distribution to all the people of the goods and services produced by all the people," and—in *sixth place*—a comprehensive system of social security.

Radical Planism said, in essence, that *Canada* itself had interests that conflicted with liberal acquisitive individualism. The existing Canadian state, if made responsive to a nationalistic agenda, could be a significant agent of change. Working within the system was the realistic and appropriate option for those who wanted to explore its egalitarian limits. The overtones of Fabian gradualism are obvious. What has been less obvious is that this was a relatively new emphasis on the Canadian left.[20]

Once again, then, come the questions.

- What is the purpose of left-wing activity? It is the achievement of a planning state that will draw upon the expertise of professional social science to intervene scientifically in the business cycle, socialize massive amounts of the economy, equalize life opportunities as much as possible, and achieve a genuine Canadian independence.
- What, then, is socialism? It is the planned society, in which the state serves the interests of all. More specifically, being a socialist means immersing oneself in the political process as it stands. Socialism is about state ownership—the expansion of the non-capitalist sectors of the economy—under the leadership of a professionally trained cadre of experts answerable to parliament.
- Who are the most important agents in struggling for socialism? Middle-class professionals, farmers, fishermen, the "labour movement"—all who share an interest in an enlightened planning state.
- What are the political structures of the formation? The mass electoral party, which places an emphasis, unprecedented on the left, on the achievement of parliamentary power as an intrinsic, even crucial aspect of left struggle. A further characteristic form is the organic union of the party and the labour bureaucracy, achieved in part through the automatic checkoff of union dues, some of them funnelled to the party coffers.
- What are the major characteristics that distinguish this formation from others? To a degree unequalled by its predecessors, it is able to speak a socialism with which many producers can identify and that integrates

important elements of the Social Gospel. The 1944 victory in Saskatchewan gave the CCF important regional and national credentials—now a provincial government could be cited as a realistic model of "living otherwise," which, as it evolved, did not seem to require Canadians to undergo a complete cultural revolution.

It was thanks to this formation of state-building leftists that "socialism" came to be written, although not in indelible ink, into some of the core myths and symbols of postwar Canadian nationalism. If the lasting achievement of the revolutionaries was their role in the creation of the great trade unions that have been such a force for social justice in Canada, the enduring achievement of the radical planners was to rewrite Canadian nationalism—essentially moving Canada's complex of myths and symbols from one associated closely with a decaying empire to one that emphasized egalitarianism, social equality, and peace. (It is a testament to their success that these are now often simply referred to, even by Liberal Party supporters, as "Canadian values.") Saskatchewan came to be an exemplar, not of some sinister alien radicalism, but of "Canadianism." There came to be a profound third formation identification with renovating the liberal order, focusing especially on the government in Ottawa as the proper carrier of socialist hopes and dreams. In sharp contrast to their marginalized comrades in the United States, third formation socialists could tell themselves that they were shaping a new Canadian state for a new Canadian people. The realm of freedom glimpsed in *Make This Your Canada*—a Canadian society in which the average person is freed from economic insecurity and therefore able to enjoy a much more fulfilling life—is one that still resonates in Canadian public life.

In addition to taking note of this immense achievement, a reconnaissance would also need to evaluate those factors contributing to the assimilation of the formation by the liberal order. Externally, the Cold War, especially played out in a country acutely vulnerable to even the slightest changes in U.S. strategy, made CCFers ever more reluctant to project ideas that could be tagged as communistic. The conceptual system of the third formation was much more indebted to non-socialist intellectuals—Keynes most obviously—than were the formations that went before it, which made it all the more vulnerable to a politics of passive revolution. Aspects internal to the third formation contributed to this pattern. Neither a "propaganda party" nor a "vanguard party," the CCF marginalized the earlier emphasis that socialists had placed on education. There was throughout the time of the third formation a greatly reduced interest in a holistic critique of capitalism. Reliance on the labour bureaucracy as a key source of members and money meant a withering away of the grassroots democracy championed by the radicals in the party—the "political check-off" proved to be a powerful force in changing the prospects of Canadian socialism. Creating a bureaucratic "socialism of administration" meant, perhaps inevitably, that the CCF planners sounded much like liberal planners. The fervent nationalism of the third wave marked an audacious attempt to articulate what Gramsci would call a "national-popular will," a new historic bloc of the "people of Canada." In the absence of a detailed working through of the country's three-part national question, however, the third formation formulas had remarkably little to offer anyone who could not identity with a centralizing state in Ottawa. Their wholehearted identification with the liberal state institutions that had originated in the era of British rule meant that third formationists could scarcely conduct constructive conversations with leftisms that called the legitimacy of those very institutions into question.

NEW LEFTISTS AND LIBERATION

In the 1960s and 1970s a fourth left formation emerged, responding to the Cold War and, more generally, to the decolonization movements that were shaking the entire globe. Internationally, the break between the "Old Left" and the "New Left" was registered with a massive outpouring of publications and the near-revolutions that occurred in 1968, most dramatically in France. New Leftists declared their opposition to both an "obsolete communism" and a "sold-out social democracy." They demanded a new politics of resistance founded on authentic emancipation and human freedom, a "socialism" of self-management, anti-imperialism, and direct democracy. They too produced a "Marx," but—thanks to recent discoveries—this was more often the passionate democrat, the "Young Marx," than the sober scientist of *Capital*.

In contrast to the first three formations, the New Left was less likely to focus primarily on the exploitation of the working class in production, for a whole new horizon of liberation was opening up before the eyes of the young radicals: the left's critical vision ranged from the oppressive world of the family as it had been explored by Freud and his more radical followers to the power of "race" as a source of oppression in struggles that spanned the globe, from Algeria—this was the era of Frantz Fanon—to the U.S. South. In contrast to the revolutionary proletarian dictatorship envisaged by the likes of Maurice Spector, or the comprehensive planning state imagined by David Lewis and F.R. Scott, the New Leftists proposed more participatory, consensual, and anti-hierarchical forms of democracy. The goal was a fully transformed society, the antithesis of the bourgeois liberal order, a future in which men and women had overcome their alienation and achieved a realm of freedom.

If, for some, concepts developed within older languages of socialism were still at work, they were now functioning in a different way—as *anticipatory forms* of a humanistic, emancipated society (and not, as before, signifying the *functional requirements* of systemic change). Institutionally, this was the formation that popularized the concept of a decentred movement of movements. Some of the members of this formation could still make a personal investment in the CPC or NDP. But for many, the truly counter-hegemonic elements in the left were new configurations—the Student Union for Peace Action, the Student Christian Movement, the Canadian Union of Students, the ambiguous Company of Young Canadians, and so on—that were only notionally fighting for the same post-capitalist future. It was, finally, a formation demarcated as never before by the concept of *youth politics*: revealingly, the leading anglophone theoretical journal of this formation was a Montreal publication called *Our Generation*.[21]

If much of the Canadian New Left would look familiar to most students of the phenomenon worldwide, in one respect the rise of this fourth formation reshaped the entire field of Canadian politics. New Leftism and left nationalism coincided to contribute to a profound crisis of Canada itself.

Historians of Canadian socialism have conveyed a sense of francophone Quebec as being generally marginal to the organized socialist movement before 1960, but that is not entirely the case. The three earlier formations had prominent Québécois supporters: Albert Saint-Martin, the SPC's Montreal militant and founder of the L'Université Ouvrière; Henri Gagnon, an impressive Communist writer and theorist whose fierce anti-homelessness activism in Montreal won continental renown in the late 1940s and should today be an inspiration to anti-poverty activists; and Thérèse Casgrain, pioneering feminist and the CCF's Quebec leader, are prime examples. Yet few would also dispute that Québécois were underrepresented in the first three formations. A major difference after 1960, and a seismic shift in the landscape of Canadian politics to this day, was that Québécois would henceforth be overrepresented on the left. Were it not for Quebec, wherein this fourth great moment of the left has been preserved, even if in attenuated form, Canada might well have succumbed to the wave of right-wing irrationalism that has engulfed so much of the rest of the North Atlantic world.

After 1960 Montreal became the storm centre of New Left politics in Canada, and therein lies a paradox. The New Leftism of Montreal unfolded on what was still formally Canadian territory, but (for many participants) often in a post-Canadian, Québécois "imagined" realm of decolonized freedom. The application to Canada of the themes of anti-colonialism meant that the very Canadian state that CCFers had so radically wanted to expand—as the epicentre and guarantee of their realm of freedom—Quebec nationalists wanted to overthrow. New Leftists in francophone Montreal often assumed that Québec was a *nation*, and not a province; that the Québécois were "the people" to whom leftists should address themselves. Since its inception Canadian socialism had (generally) blithely neglected the national questions. In the late twentieth century, the bill for this disinterest came due, and with compound interest.

The Quiet Revolution was influenced by many things: for instance, Vatican II, which liberated Catholics to pursue more progressive expressions of their faith; the mass mobilization of a freshly organized labour movement, which would become the most radical on the continent; and the rise of a technocratic middle class. To these conventional factors (cited in most books about the Quiet Revolution), a reconnaissance of its New Left aspects would add the new openness of Quebec to the French left and the reception of the French Revolution of May 1968, those miraculous days when Paris suddenly reclaimed its great stature as the world capital of enlightenment and revolutionary reason. Such a reconnaissance, whose outlines can only be sketched here, would also take note that the relative weakness of the earlier formations on Quebec soil had its positive side. These earlier formations, if they had been stronger, might arguably have diverted New Leftism into other channels (as was perhaps the case with the NDP in much of anglophone Canada). It is in this specific Quebec-centred sense that New Leftism, far from being marginal to the history of Canadian socialism, has on the contrary defined many of its postwar features. In a thousand ways the very New Leftism that elsewhere has been buried and gone haunts Canadians still, a radiant moment, even if shadowed by unnecessary and self-destructive violence, of inspiration and people's power.

The "red decades" opened in the early 1960s in Montreal and wound down in the early 1980s. These were years in which a new Québécois nationalism gained tremendous strength, culminating in the election of a social-democratic Parti Québécois (PQ) government in 1976 and the holding of the first sovereignty-association referendum in 1980. Louis Fournier's excellent chronology of this period describes sixteen revolutionary and semi-revolutionary groups active in Montreal from 1960 to 1968. Not just a thriving left-wing press but also a mass media alive with neo-Marxist and *indépendantiste* ideas testified to a socialist cultural ferment unparalleled in Canadian left history except by the radical labour upsurge of 1917–22. *Gauchistes* were generally determined to fuse international leftism (associated in Montreal with Frantz Fanon and Albert Memmi, the latter resident for a time in the city) with the particularities of the Quebec struggle.

These years are often too simply read as being only about the national question in Quebec, when for many key leftists prior allegiance to a world revolutionary process was assumed. The point of Quebec's independence was not to perpetuate liberal order and capitalist social relations in a separate Quebec: it was to liberate part of the planet from U.S. and Canadian capitalist domination—much as the Vietnamese and Cubans were fighting to do in their heroic struggles with the government (not the people) of the United States. *Nègres blancs d'amérique*, the passionate first-person reminiscence and manifesto on the liberation of Quebec by Pierre Vallières, Front de Libération du Québec (FLQ) theorist, was even in its title concerned to make the point that the struggle of the working-class Québécois was only meaningful if it was seen as part of a world struggle.[22]

In English Canada the rise of New Leftism also raised the spectre of the national question. In the late 1960s a significant number of New Democrats came together to form what came to be known as the Waffle movement. Their Manifesto—although defeated in 1969 at an unimaginative Winnipeg meeting of the party—came to stand for the most radical aspirations of New Democrats who had been moved by the New Left, the struggle against the War in Vietnam, and the women's movement. Breaking clearly with the third formation emphasis on renovating the liberal state and focusing strictly on the parliamentary party, the Waffle Manifesto called for a new vision of the left party as only one element within a renovated socialist formation. "The achievement of socialism awaits the building of a mass base of socialists in factories and offices, on farms and campuses. The development of socialist consciousness, on which can be built a socialist base, must be the first priority of the New Democratic Party," the Manifesto declared. "The New Democratic Party must be seen as the parliamentary wing of a movement dedicated to fundamental social change. It must be radicalized from within and it must be radicalized from without."[23] The Wafflers were purged from the Ontario party in 1972. Some of the members attempted to become an independent group, the Movement for an Independent Socialist Canada (and a remnant persisted as "the Waffle" in Saskatchewan). Many of the Waffle's left-nationalist ideas were nonetheless influential, especially when the federal Liberals were reduced to a minority government in the 1970s, leaving the NDP with the balance of power. Under the co-leadership of James Laxer, who had studied the Quebec question in some detail, the Waffle also struggled to defend self-determination for Quebec as a fundamental principle of the entire Canadian left.[24]

To sum up the fourth formation, inevitably too briefly and too crudely, we can once again pose our leading questions.

- What is the purpose of left-wing activity? It is to create anticipations of a realm of freedom in the here and now, liberating men and women from the deadening alienation and ambient dread of liberal capitalist order.
- What, then, is socialism? The liberated society dreamt of by the New Left—only sometimes covered by the rubric of "socialism"—is a radical democracy characterized by workers' control of production, the end of consumerism, even (in the ecstatic utopianism of Vallières, an inspired and tragic figure) the *disappearance* of money itself. Its vision of a realm of freedom includes de-alienated men and women who, no longer enslaved to routine, no longer bound to a narrow individualism, no longer psychologically frustrated, no

longer lacking in confidence in their own revolutionary possibilities, can remake the world.

- Who are the most important agents in struggling for socialism? Some in the fourth formation would still say, "the working class." Yet perhaps the majority would say racial minorities, the young, the oppressed nations—the "people" struggling against imperialism, in the rice paddies of Vietnam, the ghettoes of the United States, and the streets of Montreal.
- What are the political structures of the formation? Some of the activity takes place within the conventional parties—the New Democratic Youth was for a time a major focal point of New Leftism—but the organizational signature of this formation is the often ad hoc, spontaneous group organized around a specific issue (such as the massive movement aimed at ending Canada's complicity in the war in Vietnam).
- What are some of the major characteristics that distinguish this formation from others? In speaking to the spiritual and psychological suffering involved in late capitalism—*Nègres blancs* would have mystified an earlier generation of radicals with its discussion of sexuality, child/parent relationships, the emptiness of life under conditions of modernity—the New Leftists name problems that, on the left, had long gone without names. (To bring back our old analogy: some new cards—the politics of emancipated sexuality, the exaltation of "the moment"—were at play in this game that had never been central before in the politics of the Canadian left.) After the 1960s and 1970s, the national oppression of the Québécois, long a well-disguised secret of liberal order, could no longer be evaded by any left purporting to address the country as a whole.

Yet the split on the left along national lines, along with the earlier identification of the CCFers with the strengthening of the federal state, meant that there was unlikely to be a strong pan-Canadian left that could carry on this work. In the 1960s and 1970s there opened a chasm—political and cultural—between two left traditions, a chasm that has persisted to this day. To a degree unprecedented by its predecessors, not only did the fourth formation speak a language of youthful protest against the inherent irrationality and cruelty of capitalism, but it also generally found it difficult to build on this critique a movement that could establish a substantial popular base—except in Quebec. That province would to a significant extent be the major place in North America where, fusing with popular nationalism, New Leftism was able to exert an enduring and powerful influence. Any history of the Quebec left must take account of three great labour institutions—the Centrale de l'enseignement du Québec (CEQ), Confédération des syndicats nationaux (CSN), and Fédération de travail du Québec (FTQ)—and their coming together in the early 1970s to form the Common Front, an event that profoundly influenced the vision of the left.[25]

The enduring contribution of the fourth formation was to write into the collective imagination of Quebec, with enduring implications for all of Canada, the central significance of social solidarity. No less than in English Canada, but in markedly different ways, did the concept of a social-democratic planning state become intertwined with questions of national survival. The election of the Parti Québécois in 1976, a government that included, especially in its first administration, a large number of leftists, has had an enduring impact on the province. Few would ever define the Parti Québécois of today as a socialist party, and yet there is something of "living otherwise" in many ideas about sovereignty. In some cases, "sovereignty" and "socialism" came to appear as synonyms in the mouths of those who dreamed a big dream of a Quebec that could breathe free, *and in French*, a Quebec of equal citizens, of social justice, of inclusiveness and generosity. The Quebec population, once viewed by the political scientist and civil servant O.D. Skelton as one of the great barriers that would shield a fortunate Canada from the waves of socialism sweeping the world, has helped to safeguard the entire country from being swept up by the right-wing crazes so evident in less fortunate lands. One of the more delicious ironies of contemporary Canada is that Canada's "independence" from reckless schemes of integration with the United States is safeguarded by a solid phalanx of sovereigntist MPs who are, at least in theory, supposed to be dismantling the country. Skelton must be turning in his grave—in company with several generations of clerical nationalists, for whom socialism was always so anathema.[26]

SOCIALIST FEMINISTS AND EQUALITY

A fifth formation, socialist feminism, arose around 1966 and lasted into the 1990s. It was part of a massive worldwide movement of women rising up against their oppression. One important founding text was a paper, "Brothers, Sisters, Lovers . . . Listen . . ." presented in 1967 to a meeting of the Student Union for

Peace Action, a leading force of Canadian New Leftism in the 1960s.[27] The paper began almost apologetically. "We hope that it will not be taken as vindictive, but that certain directions may come from this discussion. Believing as Marx does that 'social progress can be measured by the social position of the female sex,' we will attempt to describe the human condition in New Left terms as it exists today." Its authors, recently allied with the Toronto Women's Liberation Group, articulated a new radicalism, which in effect refused the subordination of women in society and of sexism within the left. Their Manifesto marked a moment, 1966–68, that we can cite as the beginning of a new kind of leftism in Canada.

The Manifesto of 1967 announces—it did not itself quite inaugurate—the opening of a new socialist formation in Canada. The matrix-event was a vast postwar change throughout Western countries in the economic and social position of women. The feminization of women's employment, the achievement of the Keynesian welfare state, the unforetold and unprecedented demographic and personal changes that followed the diffusion and legitimization of contraception, the erosion of religious prohibitions against the equality of women, an international rights movement in which the individuality of women was generally recognized: these and other changes constituted a women's revolution that inescapably transformed the socialist left. A fifth, and in some respects the most radical, moment of supersedure called into question the very categories of "men" and "women" through which so much conventional experience and practice were—and still are—organized.

The moment of supersedure can be boiled down to a few sentences. Throughout the world and throughout most recorded history, women have been oppressed by men. They still are today. They are denied their full humanity by capitalist labour markets, in which they are paid less than men are for work of equal value—and not paid at all for their indispensable and often compulsory labour in the household, where they reproduce the labour-power of the future. They are equally oppressed by liberal definitions of individualism, classically designed with free-standing males in mind. In a liberal polity, women are formally the equals, but actually the inferiors, of men. Women are denied access not only to power, but also to respect and physical safety, and the old liberal formula of a division between "the political" and "the personal" works to disguise this fact. Women are, collectively, a dominated and oppressed group, and without their emancipation, any general scheme for human betterment, no matter how revolutionary it sounds, will simply perpetuate old patterns of oppression. Its universal categories will simply cause women to disappear from view.

This struggle was complex. The "longest revolution" of women against male domination, analyzed by Juliet Mitchell in an important and intensely read *New Left Review* article of 1966, was complicated by the existence of the earlier socialist approaches to revolutionary activism. None could be either straightforwardly rejected or accepted. The New Left emphases on authenticity, spontaneity, and radical democracy were carried forward into the new moment—the very name of "women's liberation," which was generally applied in the earliest years of this formation, echoed the many other liberation movements that New Leftists were saluting throughout the globe, from Algeria to Vietnam. But in many other respects the feminist revolution was the negation of the New Left negation of liberal order. It performed what some Marxist scholars call an "immanent critique"—a critique from within—which condemned the sexism that, unconsciously or otherwise, persisted in a supposedly anti-hierarchical radicalism. Weren't many New Leftists simply another crop of self-serving male leaders? Had they not taken doctrines of sexual liberation as permission slips to act out their fantasies with impunity?

Other formations were similarly critiqued. Working backwards, through the prior formations: the actually existing "state socialisms" of communism and social democracy certainly drew some support among women in the new formation, many of whom would gravitate to old and new vanguard parties or to the NDP's Waffle faction. But over time socialist feminists would develop a far different, more sceptical and pragmatic, stance towards "the state" than was to be found in either the CCF or the CPC. Not only would the Canadian state engage in the strategies of passive revolution, conceding the minimum of the feminist program in order to contain this moment within the liberal-capitalist institutional framework; but it would also address only a fraction of the issues that feminists saw as being most important. As well, attempts to "utopianize" the achievements of women in socialist countries abroad—however defined—no longer convinced these women.

As for the legacy of the socialist revolutionaries, its impact was if anything more contradictory. From 1965 to 1990 many socialist feminists of all persuasions—from the initial women's liberationists through those working to integrate Marxism and feminism to those seeking to recoup Marxism's revolutionary legacy in a free-standing feminist politics—would have described themselves as revolutionaries who identified strongly with the revolutionary-utopian side of Marxism. But when they came to consider more closely the actual legacy of revolutionary Marxism, many socialist feminists experienced a kind of visceral repugnance—not only against the transparent exaltation of male power and privilege in Marxists texts and symbols, but also against the textual authority and epistemological absolutism of the (actually existing) Leninist versions of "scientific method."

Finally, when they came to consider the nineteenth- and early twentieth-century texts of the socialist formation based on evolutionary theory, many feminist activists were initially quite inspired by the openness to the woman question of such heavy-duty theorists as Engels and the German Social Democrat August Bebel, by the concept of a matriarchal prehistory, and by the extensive writings of socialist-feminist figures. Within the first formation one could find—surprisingly—elements of an empowering narrative of the inevitability and necessity of women's liberation. But this early-1970s enthusiasm was followed by a more critical late-1970s reading, to which Canadian feminists made especially original and substantial contributions. These drew out the class- and race-based specificity of much of this earlier feminism, as well as its ultimate reliance upon a master evolutionary narrative—from matriarchy to patriarchy to equality—that came to seem less and less plausible in the light of empirical and theoretical reflection.[28]

To become a socialist feminist meant to struggle both within and against many of the received ideas of the socialist tradition. It simultaneously meant to struggle within and against feminists who identified themselves with incremental reforms within the liberal order, who focused on questions of personal fulfilment, and who felt no sense of being part of a more general radical movement. Within socialism and within feminism, socialist feminists were thus engaged in a two-front struggle: against (and alongside) socialists, who had so often spoken a language of universal interests when what they really meant were male heterosexual interests, and against (and alongside) liberal feminists, who had so often spoken of women's advancement without probing the material preconditions and class interests of a revived women's movement. Those who fully inhabited the position of socialist feminism were not so much socialists who happened to be feminists, or feminists with a social conscience, but theorists and activists fired by radically distinctive visions of both feminism and socialism alike. The woman question, long a peripheral concern in the Canadian socialist movement, became a central preoccupation of many Canadian leftists. When women themselves started asking hard questions about the traditions purporting to hold out the prospects of their liberation, the answers started to look quite different than they ever had before.[29]

The "longest revolution" transformed the social and cultural landscape of post-1960 Canada. Merely to list some of feminism's obvious achievements—the coming of employment equity; the massive organization of women in trade unions and their rise to positions of leadership within them; the rise of socialist feminism to a position of ideological centrality within the New Democratic Party; the phenomenal growth of scholarship focused on women, especially in the social sciences and humanities; the organization of a campaign against male violence against women and for shelters to care for its victims; the general acceptance that abortion is a question to be decided by a woman advised by her doctor—is to suggest the magnitude of the women's revolution that unfolded from 1965 to 1990. But even this list of developments underestimates the scope of the change. What feminism achieved was a massive re-evaluation of existing beliefs and practices formerly taken to be natural rather than historical. What Canadian socialist feminists also succeeded in doing was to articulate this massive sea-change in sensibility to the specific circumstances of Canada, thereby shaping a movement that was distinctive in the world. It was a classic example of a new counter-hegemony, which both borrowed from and deeply resisted a surrounding liberal order.[30]

The suddenness and scope of the moment of women's liberation were startling. In 1960 few watchers of the political scene would have anticipated the full-scale eruption that was unquestionably in evidence ten years later. A remarkable surge of activism and influence occurred after 1968. In that year a women's caucus of the Students for a Democratic Union at the University of Toronto quickly blossomed into the largely off-campus Working Women's Association. A similar development took place in Vancouver. The fall of 1968 saw the formation of the Toronto Women's Liberation Movement, followed in the late 1960s by Saskatoon Women's Liberation, which is sometimes listed as the first self-declared socialist-feminist organization.[31]

In 1969 an important Western Women's Liberation Conference was held in Vancouver, and an equally important transformation occurred in Toronto with the emergence of the New Feminists, who saw themselves as taking "Women's Liberation" to its next, more radical level. In 1970 women's liberation movements took root in Regina and Fredericton. In Toronto the Leila Khaled Collective sought to integrate the struggle of women with those of the colonized peoples of the globe; and the Toronto Women's Caucus, in conjunction with the Vancouver Women's Caucus, threw itself into a struggle against abortion laws in which Trotskyists, Communists, and left-wing members of the NDP all took part. At the same time Saskatoon hosted the first national congress of the radical women's movement. The appointment of a Royal Commission on the Status of Women was one sure indication that the governing Liberals now saw it as important to appear to be responding to women's demands. In 1972 the Commission's *Report* was released—and although the left massively critiqued it as an example of lame liberalism, the publicity that it generated across the country, the research it legitimated, and the liberal radicalism of some of its proposals suggest that it bore all the contradictory marks of an attempt to forestall feminism's more revolutionary articulation.[32]

Its most permanent outcome would be the establishment of the National Action Committee on the Status of Women (NAC), a body through which many socialist feminists could influence women sympathetic to, but not fully integrated into, the new socialist paradigm. In 1973 the first women's bookstore in Canada opened in Vancouver, and the Wages for Housework campaign became highly influential in Toronto and elsewhere. In 1977 and 1978 there was a mounting struggle against violence against women, entailing direct action against pornography retailers and the formation of Women Against Violence Against Women in Toronto. In 1979 the Feminist Party of Canada was launched; it would remain a political presence, especially within feminist circles in Toronto, for about two years. A different articulation was the increasingly overt socialist-feminist movement, typified by the Bread and Roses Collective in Vancouver, formed in 1980.

Having influenced much of the earlier Waffle movement in the early 1970s, socialist feminists attained positions of power within the NDP in the following decade. Such was the new prominence of the fifth formation that when the senior federal and provincial politicians and bureaucrats contemplated changing the Constitution without listening to feminist women, they could be swiftly called to order by a powerful, vibrant women's network. During the federal election of 1988 the party leaders, all male, were even required to participate in a debate specifically focused on the demands of women. That same year, after a series of trials in which Dr. Henry Morgentaler became a popular hero to abortion reformers across the country, the Supreme Court declared the abortion law unconstitutional. The issue that had brought thousands into the streets in the early 1970s ended with a clear-cut feminist victory—one that contemporary polls suggest will be very difficult for the Canadian right to reverse. By the 1990s the network of feminist movements, many of them attached to NAC, constituted one of the most important forces of the Canadian left. In the end, no list of "headline events" can capture the depth and seriousness of the rise of left feminism, which unfolded as powerfully and permanently on the small stages of personal lives as it did in the great forums of national politics.

Few would dispute the world-changing impact of modern feminism. How the moment should be described and its many debates analyzed, though, are highly controversial. One commonly accepted typology distinguishes among competing trends of "socialist feminism," "radical feminism," and "liberal feminism." These categories are useful at a general level, but for the purpose of reconnaissance they can too easily lead analysis astray. One difficulty with this typology is that these terms designate forces of radically unequal power. A "liberal feminism," which accepts liberal-capitalist order and seeks incremental improvements of the place of women within it, is not usefully viewed as a competitor with other feminisms. It does not share their fundamental antagonism to the existing social order and their articulation of a world that is radically otherwise; nor are its adherents required to pay the price that all leftists must pay for their dissidence from the liberal mainstream.

To the contrary, however distinctively they are formulated, feminisms that do envisage a realm of freedom beyond liberal order and capitalist social relations are too easily polarized when, for all the heat generated by their debates, they actually share substantial radical counter-hegemonic ground. Counter-liberal feminisms can and do differ in their emphases, but to the extent that they seek something other than the reform of the social given they are compelled to resemble each other more than they do liberal feminism, for the simple reason that they are pitted against an immensely powerful liberal matrix of institutions and ideas. Following from the definition of socialism that guides our inquiry, all counter-liberal feminisms in modern Canada have been socialist in the basic sense of bringing the injustices of capitalism to light and projecting a more egalitarian alternative over and against them.

A second problem with this typology is that these frameworks can be interpreted in an ahistorical way, inattentive to political context and conceptual specificity. By maximizing the clarity and absoluteness of each "camp," and tending to read into each a fixed-and-firm identity that a more refined analysis would necessarily qualify, framework analysis can be simplistic. One is tempted to divorce each from its complex relationship with the others, and from its own position in history.[33]

Most left feminisms in Canada remained in a close dialogue with Marx—much more so, and more lastingly, it would seem, than did their counterparts in either the United States or Britain. Overriding some important distinctions and subtleties, we can distil the common socialist-feminist quest to be a post-liberal democratic order in which women would be at least the equals of men. The choice of these terms assumes, against many conventional international assumptions, that all these non-liberal "threads" of feminist conversation and activism were "socialist" in a basic, non-trivial, sense. All argued that women's liberation required the emancipation of people from an objective dependence upon things and upon alienated social forces. All contested any approach that would be satisfied with selective reforms, individual success stories, or parliamentary politics. All wanted a comprehensive otherwise to capitalist society and liberal order. And—more radically—all of them overlapped in their arguments.

The rise of second-wave feminism, like that of the first wave, was also conditioned by the social and economic context within which it occurred—the growing feminization of non-domestic labour, the rise of the service sector to economic predominance, the mushrooming of suburbia and the rapid decline of the rural population, the exponential expansion of the universities and the growing size of their female student bodies, the unprecedented rise in the standard of living, state macro-economic planning, and the widespread legitimation of the social welfare state. To these "objective conditions" must be added the "subjective reality" of the ideal of the postwar citizen. This new democratic ideal went beyond the negative freedoms sanctioned by classical liberalism to the positive freedoms of social security, educational growth, and even spiritual development.[34]

Equipped with the standard-issue Marxist tool kit, the early orthodox critics of the women's revolution had no difficulty reducing the movement to its "bourgeois" social origins. Such orthodox critics did not appreciate the irony of their own hasty conclusion, because exactly the same things had been said, and with equal accuracy, about most socialist thinkers of the past—who were not disqualified by their middle-class origins from making a substantial impact on history. Canadian nationalists might also point to the U.S. origins of some of feminism's most articulate advocates, particularly in Toronto. But here again, every previous socialist formation had followed this pattern: a first stage of intensive international borrowing from abroad, followed by an equally intense moment of Canadianization. There was a further irony: in some respects feminism was far more "organic" to the massive socio-economic change ushered in by the post-war socio-economic formation than were the traditional labour-based ideologies of the left. The mid-1970s provides an approximate death-date for the golden age of the welfare state, with the simultaneous advent of a new world economic order and the beginning of the decline of state programs (and not coincidentally of the organized political strength of the male-dominated trade unionists). Socialist feminists—more strongly rooted in the labour movement than either contemporary feminists or most subsequent historians have allowed—could now present themselves as being more connected with what was actually happening within a rapidly feminizing working class itself than were conventional Marxists. All these changes represented a comeuppance for orthodox Marxists, who had once been so swift with their base-and-superstructure dismissals of the supposedly "bourgeois" feminist movement. In the choice between what Gramsci termed "historical economism" and "historical materialism," such diehards still opted for the former. Such choices are unfortunate in most contexts; they were fatally misleading in this one. They prevented many Marxists from integrating into their own understanding the core socialist-feminist moment of supersedure: no worthwhile historical materialism can neglect the dialectical interaction of *production* and *reproduction*—and *reproduction* not just in the economic sense that Marx develops in *Capital*, but also in the fullest social and natural sense that we find in the young Marx's anthropology of human nature.[35]

Roberta Hamilton and Michèle Barrett have insightfully suggested that one distinctive Canadian pattern—evident as early as the publication of *Women Unite!* of 1972—was the extensive prior involvement by Canadian feminists in the socialist movement.[36] Into the 1980s, feminists would remark on the differences setting the Canadian climate apart from that in England or the United States. Lorna Weir, for example, observed that, when travelling abroad, Canadian socialist feminists were often surprised "to discover the strongly academic and weakly activist formation of socialist feminism in these countries."[37] Socialist feminists in Canada were less centred on academia and more on popular movements. In Canada there seemed to be, apart from some who remained with the Leninist parties and others who gravitated to more mainstream feminist formations, a much more stable socialist-feminist centre. Here the Canadian feminist left probably derived some advantages from the peculiar status of the NDP.

The presence of a social democratic party—distant enough from office to attract idealists, close enough to make a real difference in the lives of women—meant that much activism influenced by socialist feminism unfolded within the NDP. It would hardly be an exaggeration to identify this element as one of the ideologically most salient forces acting on the party in the 1980s and 1990s. Memories of the left-nationalist Waffle often emphasize the particular theoretical and organizational significance of the many socialist feminists active in it; they pushed the NDP to adopt gender parity in key committees and to take more aggressively pro-feminist stances at tumultuous conventions in the 1970s. Many standard-issue rebuttals of U.S. exceptionalism—basically answering the perennial question, "Why is there no effective socialist party in the United States?" with the answer, "Well, so what?"—miss the centrality to socialist feminism of a large left party, close enough to power on the provincial level to make a difference to the lives of women, and distant enough from power not to have sacrificed all of its idealism in the pursuit of power. In Canada, many socialist feminists could work comfortably in the NDP.

It was much the same story with social democracy in Quebec. Whatever the unprecedented openness of the somewhat left-leaning early PQ governments to feminist arguments, this did not preclude the adoption of a pro-natalist stance reminiscent of earlier maternalist formulations of woman as mother of the nation. Yet PQ women were among the most forceful and articulate of the party's members, and it would have been unthinkable for the party to propose a return to the *ancien régime* for women.

Measured in terms of formal free-standing political structures, socialist feminism was a minor tendency. Evaluated in terms of its impact on the NDP, trade unions, and the academy, it has been a major formative influence on Canadian politics. It was undoubtedly one of the most important factors shaping left-wing politics over the last two decades of the twentieth century.

The radicalization of the National Action Committee on the Status of Women and the rise to its leadership of Judy Rebick, the advance of socialist feminists in the trade union movement, and particularly the impact of socialist feminism on the New Democratic Party, where it arguably constituted one of the most influential doctrinal poles in debates through the 1980s and 1990s: all of these elements meant that socialist feminism was not a minor ideological aberration in an irrelevant movement. Those sympathetic to it held powerful positions, and achieved a widespread public recognition, which they still enjoy. It could be that socialist feminists were the beneficiaries of both the left's weakness and its strength. They benefited from its weakness, in that established socialists—the male leftists of feminist polemics—were rarely in a position to monopolize discussions. But they also benefited from its strength, as a resurgent left within social democracy often drew upon socialist feminism as an ideological resource.

Socialist feminism in a broad sense was and remains one of the most influential currents in the NDP. It also largely revolutionized the mainstream Canadian labour movement, which—because it was generally persuaded to rethink its historic sexism in the 1980s—became far more effectively integrated with women's struggles. Socialist feminism also became one of the most influential currents within a burgeoning academy—women's studies programs, controversial newcomers on the university scene in the 1970s, are now established parts of the academic landscape. Socialist feminism demonstrated that, in the absence of a hierarchical party and a canon of approved texts, a left liberation movement could nonetheless make an enormous difference. It could fight—it may well indeed provide the most compelling historical example of—a war of position. It exemplifies, perhaps better than any other formation, the design of a Canadian leftism that initially looked like a carbon copy of movements elsewhere—but which then developed its own distinctive patterns.

Asking our standard questions again brings out what was distinctive about the leftism of the fifth formation.

- What is the purpose of left-wing activity? The empowerment of women—the liberation of women from patriarchal oppression.
- What, then, is socialism? Socialist-feminist visions of the realm of freedom extrapolate from those intense solidarities that women experience in the depths of their fierce struggles for abortion rights, against violence, and on a host of equity issues. In the socialist-feminist realm of freedom, production and reproduction are equally important.
- Who are the most important agents in struggling for socialism? Women who have become conscious of their oppression.
- What are the political structures of the formation? Some of its political forms are reminiscent of other formations—such as the Feminist Party of Canada, which briefly sought to mobilize support for the Canadian equivalent of the Women's Party in Iceland—but many are peculiar to socialist feminism itself. The National Action Committee on the Status of Women is a particularly Canadian form that combines state funding with a federation of hundreds of women's groups. It gradually became a high-profile forum for the articulation of

feminist approaches to national politics. Within the NDP, feminist caucuses became increasingly important through the 1980s, to the point, in some provinces, of setting the policy agenda. A distinctive feature of Canadian left feminism is its solid connection with the trade union movement; three of the most prominent radical trade unionists of the late twentieth century, Nancy Ritchie, Grace Hartmann, and Judy Darcy, have deep roots in left feminism. (At the risk of overgeneralization, I do not think women labour leaders of their stature, or their prominence, exist in many other North Atlantic countries.)

- What are the major characteristics that distinguish this formation from others? It focuses attention on gendered forms of power that the other formations had not theorized or acted upon. It largely reinvents "Marx" by scrutinizing, and then largely abandoning, the orthodox historical-materialist account of women's history. It is much less tied to specific institutions and much more committed to an anticipatory politics. Gender equality is not merely a projection from a distant future, but an ideal that should be lived in the everyday world, inside the trade unions, the liberal academy, and—most controversially—in the privacy of the domestic realm. In addition to the great bulwark of Quebec, the survival of much of the left through much of the dismal late 1980s and 1990s owed a great deal to the tenacity of socialist feminists, who fought tooth and nail to resist the backlash from the ominously reinvigorated extreme right.

It is perhaps too soon to write with any confidence of the waning of socialist feminism in its distinctive

Canadian variant, except to report that those central to crafting the formation themselves report a general sense of decline. In this case as in so many others, a complete reconnaissance would pay close attention to the passive-revolutionary strategies of the liberal state. In the case of feminism, the Liberal Party was able to present itself—not without a strong push from women—as an enlightened party favouring women's equality. Many socialist feminists entered the academy, where much energy was consumed by teaching and administration. Some of the reasons for the formation's perceived crisis in the 1990s lay in its internal tensions. Many feminists, particularly in the period 1978–85, had identified both the "We" and the "They" of feminism in essentialist terms. Since the 1990s, especially with the rise of Queer Theory, such analytical frameworks have come under intensive scrutiny from gays, lesbians, bisexuals, and trans peoples who believe that this essentialized female/male binary can in some circumstances be itself a cause of oppression. Within the 1980s and 1990s, left feminists also confronted a critique from women and men of colour, who did not see themselves reflected in some of the organizations of the movement. However Canadian historians eventually discuss the record of socialist feminism, they will be obliged to notice that it forced substantial, structural changes on liberal order—even down to the definition of marriage and the politics of the family—that rivalled those achieved by any other formation. It challenged the liberal order in a lastingly revolutionary way.

IN SEARCH OF THE NDP

Much of left history in the 1980s and 1990s was complicated by the perplexing identity of Canada's major left party, the NDP. There is a good case to be made that the NDP has always been what its CLC founders wanted it to be when they called for the party in 1956: a gathering place for "liberally minded Canadians." It would be hard to see anything particularly utopian or daring in the record of many of the NDP administrations in the West. After winning provincial office in British Columbia (1972–75), Manitoba (1969–77, 1981), and the CCF's old bastion of Saskatchewan (1971–82), the NDP in the 1980s would become a significant player in Western provincial politics—a development that qualified its earlier association with the concentration of political power in Ottawa.

In the 1980s the party rose to new heights of national popularity and representation in the House of Commons under the inspired leadership of Ed Broadbent, at one time a supporter of the Waffle Manifesto and enthusiast for Yugoslav-style grassroots socialism. In the run-up to the federal election of 1988, Broadbent led the polls in terms of political popularity and the party seemed on the verge of a breakthrough in Quebec, where it had never enjoyed much previous success. It won a good many seats, although none in Quebec, but a Liberal/NDP split allowed the victory of the right-wing Conservatives and the passage of the Free Trade Agreement. Overall, the 1988 experience was registered as a defeat.

The 1990s were generally bleak for the party. In the 1993 federal election it garnered just 939,575 votes, or a mere 6.9 per cent—a stark collapse from the 2,685,308 votes or 20.38 per cent it had won in 1988. In 1997, under the leadership of Alexa McDonough, the NDP recovered to 1.4 million votes or 11 per cent of the popular vote; but in 2000 it declined once again, to just over one million votes or 8.5 per cent of the total. Only in Nova Scotia (three seats), Manitoba (four seats), Saskatchewan (two seats), and the territories—Yukon, the Northwest Territories, and Nunavut, although they gave the party no seats—did the NDP win more than 15 per cent of the vote. It had become a party of the "outer Canada," shut out of all the largest cities except Vancouver.

On the provincial level the party surprisingly won the Ontario election in 1990, with 1.5 million votes (or 37.6 per cent) on a platform calling for public automobile insurance, among other progressive measures. Then—partly the victim of bad timing and partly the craven author of its own misfortune—the party swiftly descended into internal chaos and conflict with its trade-union supporters. In 1995 it was reduced to seventeen seats with a scant 20.6 per cent of the vote, and left behind it the unmistakable odour of a squandered opportunity. In the Ontario election of 2003 the NDP was unable to cling to official-party status with 15 per cent of the vote.

In 1996 the NDP government in British Columbia was narrowly returned to office with 39.4 per cent of the vote, but—thanks to the marvels of the first-past-the-post system—won thirty-nine seats, five more than the opposition Liberals. In 2001 it was dragged down by scandal and perceived inefficiency to a mere two seats with 21.6 per cent of the vote (the extreme-right wing Liberal Party won the other seventy-seven seats). In this election the Green Party, with 197,231 votes or 12.4 per cent of the total, provided stiff competition for the NDP, which won a mere 343,156 votes.

In the federal election of 2004 the NDP—running now on a platform that out-greened the Greens—elected nineteen members with a substantially improved vote of over 2.1 million (15.7 per cent)—not quite enough to hold the balance of power in a minority-led House of Commons, and not as high as it had been in 1988—but still a substantial recovery from its dismal record in the 1990s.[38] It would enjoy an influence unwarranted by this modest seat count by virtue of its power base in cities that the Liberal Party must win to retain power. The federal NDP now had an imaginative new leader, and to its great credit has recently stood up for the human rights of gays and lesbians. It has been the stalwart defender of the "Canadian values" enshrined in our myth-symbol complex by the CCF.

Unlike earlier left parties, the NDP is deeply implicated in the liberal order. It undertakes little systematic educational work. Although the party claims descent from the CCF, its vision lacks the system-challenging radicalism of *Make This Your Canada*. Its ideological statements generally place a vaguely "social" spin on mainstream liberal sentiments. Engaged in run-of-the-mill electoral politics, the NDP often exemplifies Mackenzie King's famous description: "Liberals in a hurry." It can be counted on to defend the general welfare state at the federal level, while at the same time fiscal stringencies may require it to cut spending and rationalize—much as any other party would do—when it holds provincial office. Nobody expects the social world to be turned upside down if an NDP government comes to power in a Canadian province.

At the same time the NDP is rather different from many mass Western social-democratic parties in the depth and tenacity of the new social movements that have found a home within it. Socialist feminists were particularly successful in influencing the party. More recently a gay and lesbian caucus has strengthened a once-wavering party in its support for the civil rights of oppressed sexual minorities (a struggle exemplified by the inspirational career of Svend Robinson). Much of the left combines a primary commitment to new social movements outside the party with some degree of involvement within it. In a Canada confronting the menace of a rogue U.S. state to the south, solid NDP commitments to peace, the environment, and human rights are bound to seem more and more attractive.

The party has even sought to become relevant—and it may yet become so—to the global justice movements that have brought thousands of young protestors into the streets of Seattle and Quebec City. In the third formation the party was often conceptualized as a "transmission belt" carrying messages from the centre to the masses. In the contemporary NDP the formula is reversed: the party is a "transmission belt" carrying many messages from extraparliamentary left movements into the centre of Canadian politics. It means that, even with its chequered history on many issues, the NDP is not likely in the near future to be abandoned by many leftists who, pragmatically, can understand the advantages of having both effective parliamentary and strong extra-parliamentary lefts. It cannot without difficulty move too far away from the new social movements that now make up a good portion of its base.[39]

In 2001 the New Politics Initiative within the NDP argued for the formation of a new party—one that would break new ground in pushing for participatory democracy, actively engage in extraparliamentary struggles, and push for more well-defined radical policies. The Initiative was defeated but much of the thinking behind it continued to influence many elements within the Party. The Initiative was largely an attempt to respond to the emergence of a sixth formation focusing especially on global justice issues. In some respects the NDP functions as a left-liberal party. In others it serves as a loose confederation wherein leftists of many descriptions can find some measure of common ground. Its future role is difficult to predict. Much will depend on how well it connects with the sixth formation, which is unfolding the banner of the "global civil society," constructing new networks of contestation and activism outside the formal boundaries of states. It already has many accomplishments to its credit.[40]

■ ■ ■

For over a century Canadian leftists have crafted five substantial formations, each identified with particular cohorts and styles of organization. Each raised a profound challenge to liberal order. Writing against the cynical grain of our age, I see in this history a pattern of stubborn and surprisingly successful resilience. We—who want to live otherwise—have crafted something special here. Canadian radicals and socialists have achieved far, far more than they often realize. Through a shrewd and radical realism they have managed to punch far above their weight in shaping national and even international politics. Although most international surveys of the left give Canada a few paragraphs, if that, the Canadian left, taken in all its divergent complexity, has crafted one of the most impressive progressive forces in the world. False modesty on this score is as useless as sentimental sectarianism. We Canadian leftists have many stories and experiences to share with the world, and possibly can even suggest models for other Western lefts struggling against neoliberal hegemony.

Many of the labels and assumptions that are customarily brought to the writing of this history, while useful in some ways, have become fetters on its further development. The Canadian left faced down the menace of the Reform Party and Canadian Alliance in the 1990s; today it faces the more subtle, possibly more pernicious, right-wing views of the Conservatives and Liberals. Neither of those parties can be counted on to defend the liberal freedoms they pretend to revere, let alone build those freedoms into democratic rights accessible to the majority. The danger remains pressing and immediate. Canadian leftists also now confront a superpower to the south that exemplifies anti-enlightenment and irrational tendencies that put the entire world in peril. Doubtless because I am writing in this conjuncture, I believe that we ought to learn some hard lessons about how we talk both about ourselves and about the thousands of fellow leftists who came before us.

One hard lesson is the lesson of revolutionary non-violence. The war of position in which we are engaged carries high stakes. It cannot be won through frontal assaults. Nor can it be won through old habits of dogmatism. False certainties and old slogans will only hurt us now. The hard lesson is that we have to give up much certainty, the better to understand and to transform—to embrace—the radical uncertainties of our existence. We need to approach our present as we approach our past—with compassionate understanding and critical empathy for all who challenge and who have challenged liberal order. We need to learn, for the first time, the many names of the left in Canada. We need to adjust our margins in theory so that in time we can abolish social margins in reality.

"Socialism," Gramsci wrote so wisely, "is not established on a particular day—it is a continuous process, a never-ending development towards a realm of freedom that is organized and controlled by the majority of the citizens."[41] If we truly learn that lesson, we may well find that as leftists we have something infinitely more precious than sentimentality and sectarianism to take with us as we move further into the twenty-first century.

Notes

One · REALMS OF FREEDOM, REALMS OF NECESSITY

1. The Canadian poverty rates are determined by Statistics Canada's "Low Income Cut-off." See *Campaign 2000, Child Poverty in Canada* (Toronto: The Campaign, 2000), citing Survey of Consumer Finances, Statistics Canada, microdata files. For the world poverty figures, see Alex Callinicos, *Equality* (Cambridge: Polity, 2000), citing United Nations World Development Report statistics. A portion of those 1.3 billion people around the world were not technically "impoverished" because they were not caught up in world market relations. Under conditions of globalization, their autonomy from capitalist social relations is not likely to last indefinitely. For the Canadian figures, see Kevin K. Lee, *Urban Poverty in Canada: A Statistical Profile* (Ottawa: Canadian Council on Social Development, 2000); and "Women's Income and Poverty," *The CCPA Monitor*, 11,2 (June 2004), 29.
2. See <www.ucsusa.org/global_environment/global_warming/index.cfm> (30 Oct. 2004) for these and other statistics, as well as "Ecological Responses to Recent Climate Change," *Nature*, March 28, 2002; Susan Klutz, Eric Hoberg, and Lydden Polley, "Global Warming and Host-Parasite Systems in the Arctic: Should We Be Concerned?" <wildlife.usask.ca/SatellitePages/iwap/abstracts/kutzb> (14 Nov. 2003); <www.commondreams.org/headlines03/1128-04> (29 Nov. 2003). For more general jargon-free information, see Dinyar Godrej, *The No-Nonsense Guide to Climate Change* (Toronto: Between the Lines, 2001).
3. See Shereen Usdin, *The No-Nonsense Guide to HIV/AIDS* (Toronto: Between the Lines, 2004).
4. I am drawing this part of the discussion from Henri Lefebvre, *Everyday Life in the Modern World*, trans. S. Rabinowich (New Brunswick, N.J.: Transaction Publishers, 1984), 89.
5. Zygmunt Bauman, *Socialism: The Active Utopia* (London: George Allen & Unwin, 1976), especially 14–15.
6. See Francis Wheen, *Karl Marx* (London: Fourth Estate, 1999), for an engaging biography—one that whets the appetite for other more scholarly studies.

7. Karl Marx, *Capital*, trans. David Fernbach, vol.3 (New York: Vintage Books, 1981), 959.
8. See, for instance, Franz J. Hinkelammert, *The Ideological Weapons of Death: A Theological Critique of Capitalism*, trans. Phillip Berryman (Maryknoll, N.Y.: Orbis Books, 1986), 52–57.
9. These points about structure and agency owe much to Lucio Colletti, whose works on Marx and Hegel were unfortunately not much heeded when they first came out in English in the 1970s. See Lucio Colletti, *From Rousseau to Lenin: Studies in Ideology and Society* (London: New Left Books, 1972).
10. Antonio Gramsci, *Il Grido del Popolo*, 4 May 1918, as cited in David Forgacs, ed., *The Antonio Gramsci Reader* (New York: New York University Press, 2000), 39.
11. Antonio Gramsci, *Selections from the Prison Notebooks*, ed. and trans. Quinton Hoare and Geoffrey Nowell-Smith (London: Lawrence and Wishart, 1971), 360.

Two · REDEFINING THE LEFT

1. Perhaps the most elegant recent text in this vein is François Furet, *The Passing of an Illusion: The Idea of Communism in the Twentieth Century*, trans. Deborah Furet (Chicago and London: University of Chicago Press, 1999).
2. Geoff Eley, *Forging Democracy: The History of the Left in Europe, 1850–2000* (Oxford: Oxford University Press, 2002), 3.
3. Early twenty-first-century aficionados of CNN will have observed that, on what passes for its public affairs broadcasting, the "left" is dominated by mainstream Democrats who in the Canadian context would rank as exponents of the centre-right.
4. The word *socialismo* apparently first appeared in writings about crime and punishment in Italy in 1765, in Ferdinando Facchinei's commentary on Beccaria's *On Crime and Punishment*. See G. de Bertier de Sauvigny, "Liberalism, Nationalism, and Socialism: The Birth of Three Words," *The Review of Politics*, 32 (1970), 147–66; Arthur E. Bestor, "The Evolution of the Socialist Vocabulary," *Journal of the History of Ideas*, 9 (1948), 259–302 (the *Oxford English Dictionary* [Clarendon Press: 1989] suggests a somewhat different early history of the word); see also Raymond Williams, *Keywords: A Vocabulary of Culture and Society* (London: Fontana, 1976). It would be a very rare socialist, for example, who exalted the divine right of kings. Yet one should not underestimate human ingenuity: one can certainly find self-proclaimed "socialists" who defended U.S. imperialist policies in Vietnam and the Middle East, on the grounds of their inherently "progressive" role. Today, one can find other self-described socialists, such as Tony Blair, who advocate the intensification of market relations in such fields as education and health.
5. Williams, *Keywords*, 286–87.

6. Margaret Cole as cited in Harry Ritter, ed., *Dictionary of Concepts in History* (1986), 418. I have found consistently helpful Michael Luntley, *The Meaning of Socialism* (London: Duckworth, 1989), especially for its discussion of the socialism/liberalism distinction (pp.9–12).
7. Karl Marx and Frederick Engels, *The Communist Manifesto* (London: Verso, 1998), an edition that includes an interesting introduction by E.J. Hobsbawm. The text may also be consulted in David McLellan, ed., *Karl Marx: Selected Writings*, 2nd ed. (Oxford: Oxford University Press, 2000), 245–72, a generally outstanding volume of Marx's writings with a good bibliographical apparatus.
8. Eley, *Forging Democracy*, 8–9.
9. Ibid., 52.
10. A general text on the "radical immigrant" is Donald Avery, *'Dangerous Foreigners': European Immigrant Workers and Labour Radicalism in Canada, 1896–1932* (Toronto: McClelland and Stewart, 1979). On the Finnish contribution to Canadian leftism, see in particular Varpu Lindström-Best's outstanding *Defiant Sisters: A Social History of the Finnish Immigrant Women in Canada, 1890–1930* (Toronto: Multicultural History Society of Ontario, 1988); and Edward W. Laine, *On the Archival Heritage of the Finnish Canadian Working-Class Movement: A Researcher's Guide and Inventory to the Finnish Organization of Canada Collection of the National Archives of Canada* (Turku, Finland: Institute of Migration, 1987).
11. For an important recent exploration of the Canadian question as seen through the lens of cultural theory, see Eva Mackey, *The House of Difference: Cultural Politics and National Identity in Canada* (London: Routledge, 1999). For an important general introduction to the resurgence of Canadian nationalism in the 1960s, see Stephen Azzi, *Walter Gordon and the Rise of Canadian Nationalism* (Montreal and Kingston: McGill-Queen's University Press, 1999). The Quiet Revolution—that complex of social and economic changes that transformed so much of Quebec society in the 1960s (some would push its boundaries earlier, and some later)—has received an imposing treatment in Pierre Godin, *La Révolution tranquille*, vol.1, *La fin de la grand noirceur*, and vol.2, *La difficile recherche de l'égalité* (Montreal: Boréal, 1991). Alain-G. Gagnon and Mary Beth Montcalm, *Quebec: Beyond the Quiet Revolution* (Toronto: Nelson Canada, 1990), is a useful guide to the remaking of Quebec; of particular interest to the historian of socialism is "The Quebec Union Movement," 78–101. For an exceptional study of two socialists who struggled hard for the rights of the Métis, see Murray Dobbin, *The One-and-a-Half Men: The Story of Jim Brady and Malcolm Norris, Metis Patriots of the 20th Century* (Regina: Gabriel Dumont Institute of Native Studies and Applied Research, 1981). F.L. Barron, *Walking in Indian Moccasins: The Native Policies of Tommy Douglas and the CCF*

(Vancouver: UBC Press, 1997), presents an interpretation less critical of the developmental vision of the CCF in Saskatchewan. For a significant breakthrough of First Nations issues into Canadian socialist thought, see Ron Bourgault, Dave Broad, Lorne Brown, and Lori Foster, eds., *1492–1992: Five Centuries of Imperialism and Resistance* (Winnipeg and Halifax: Society for Socialist Studies and Fernwood Publishing, 1992), which is stronger on continental themes than on Canadian ones.

12. Three major titles on the history of socialism and the woman's question in Canada are Janice Newton, *The Feminist Challenge to the Canadian Left 1900–1918* (Montreal and Kingston: McGill-Queen's University Press, 1995); Linda Kealey, *Enlisting Women for the Cause: Women, Labour and the Left in Canada, 1890–1920* (Toronto: University of Toronto Press, 1998), which could serve many students as a very good introduction to the entire early movement; and Joan Sangster, *Dreams of Equality: Women on the Canadian Left, 1920–1950* (Toronto: McClelland and Stewart, 1989), which is indispensable for the later period. The best secondary sources for the moment of gay liberation in Canadian left history are Tom Warner, *Never Going Back: A History of Queer Activism in Canada* (Toronto: University of Toronto Press, 2001); Miriam Smith, *Lesbian and Gay Rights in Canada: Social Movements and Equality-Seeking, 1971–1995* (Toronto: University of Toronto Press, 1999); Donald W. McLeod, *Lesbian and Gay Liberation in Canada: A Selected Annotated Chronology, 1964–1975* (Toronto: ECW Press and Homewood Books, 1996); and Didi Herman, *Rites of Passage: Struggles for Lesbian and Gay Legal Equality* (Toronto: University of Toronto Press, 1994). For an engaging profile of a pioneering gay activist, see Donald W. McLeod, comp. and ed., *Jim Egan: Challenging the Conspiracy of Silence: My Life as a Canadian Gay Activist* (Toronto: Canadian Lesbian and Gay Archives, 1998). Kathleen A. Lahey, *Are We 'Persons' Yet? Law and Sexuality in Canada* (Toronto: University of Toronto Press, 1999), surveys the changing legal landscape. Ann Silversides, *AIDS Activist: Michael Lynch and the Politics of Community* (Toronto: Between the Lines, 2003), is an outstanding portrait of an important leader.

13. On the Social Gospel, the classic discussion remains Richard Allen's rich and noteworthy *The Social Passion: Religion and Social Reform in Canada 1914–1928* (Toronto: University of Toronto Press, 1973), which remains a foundational study of the connections between religion and progressive social thought. For the religious context of turn-of-the-century Canada, see Nancy Christie and Michael Gauvreau, *A Full-Orbed Christianity: The Protestant Churches and Social Welfare in Canada, 1900–1940* (Montreal and Kingston: McGill-Queen's University Press, 1996), which challenges the view of inexorable secularization after 1900 and valuably explores debates within early "Protestant sociology" involving Spencer and his disciples. For an ambitious exploration that

describes developments in Canada, the United States, and Britain, see Paul T. Phillips, *A Kingdom on Earth: Anglo-American Social Christianity, 1880–1940* (University Park: Pennsylvania State University Press, 1996).

14. For important titles on the intellectual impact of the theory of evolution, see Carl Berger, *Science, God, and Nature in Victorian Canada* (Toronto: University of Toronto Press, 1983); and A.B. McKillop, *A Disciplined Intelligence: Critical Inquiry and Canadian Thought in the Victorian Era* (Kingston and Montreal: McGill-Queen's University Press, 1979). S.E.D. Shortt, *The Search for an Ideal* (Toronto: University of Toronto Press, 1976), examines six Canadian intellectuals as they wrestled with the challenge of capitalist modernity.
15. An important Canadian figure here is Henry Veltmeyer, whose books have reached a large international audience. See his *Development in an Era of Globalization* (London: Ashgate, 2003); and (with James Petras) *Globalization Unmasked: Imperialism in the 21st Century* (London and Halifax: Zed Press and Fernwood Publishing, 2001). The second of these texts has also been published in New Delhi (English), Madrid (Spanish), Mexico City (Spanish), Paris (French), and Rome (Italian); it is also available in Telugu and as of 2003 was being translated into Arabic, Chinese, Korean, and Hungarian. Thomas P. Socknat, *Witness against War: Pacifism in Canada, 1900–1945* (Toronto: University of Toronto Press, 1987), provides a probing analysis of the pacifist-socialist convergence in the 1930s; Barbara Roberts, "Women's Peace Activism in Canada," in *Beyond the Vote: Canadian Women and Politics*, ed. Linda Kealey and Joan Sangster (Toronto and Buffalo: University of Toronto Press, 1989), 276–308, looks at the movement from the position of women. The same author's *A Reconstructed World: Gertrude Richardson, A Biography* (1996) looks at a noteworthy socialist peace activist; and her *'Why Do Women Do Nothing to End the War?' Canadian Feminist-Pacifists and the Great War* (Ottawa: Canadian Research Institute for the Advancement of Women, CRIAW Papers, 1985), provides a fascinating overview of Richardson and three other peace activists. See also Francis Marion Beynon, *Aleta Day* (London: Virago Press, 1988 [first published 1919] for a marvellous novel about women's peace activism from the period of the First World War.
16. I draw on the discussion of Martin Kohli, "The Problem of Generations: Family, Economy, Politics," Public Lecture no.14, Institute for Advanced Study, Collegium Budapest, November 1996 <www.colbud.hu/main/PubArchiv/PL/PL14-Kohli.pdf> (19 Nov. 2003). Karl Mannheim's discussion can be found in *Essays on the Sociology of Knowledge*, ed. Paul Keckesméti (London: Routledge and Kegan Paul, 1952). Generation-specific studies in the Canadian context include Cyril Levitt, *Children of Privilege: Student Revolt in the Sixties: A Study of Student Movements in Canada, the United States, and West Germany* (Toronto: University of Toronto

Press, 1984); Doug Owram, *Born at the Right Time: A History of the Baby-Boom Generation* (Toronto: University of Toronto Press, 1996); and François Ricard, *La génération lyrique: Essai sur la vie et l'oeuvre des premiers-nés du baby-boom* (Montreal: Les Éditions du Boréal, 1994). James Laxer, *Red Diaper Baby: A Memoir* (Toronto: Douglas and McIntyre, 2004), is an interesting attempt by a prominent leftist, once in the Waffle movement, to come to terms with his parents' generation of Communists.

17. A fascinating topic that, to my knowledge, has never received its due is the radicalization of missionaries who went to such places as India and China to spread the gospel and returned to Canada as fervent socialists. Well-known peace activist J.G. Endicott is remembered in Stephen Endicott, *James G. Endicott: Rebel out of China* (Toronto: University of Toronto Press, 1980). For Mary Austin Endicott, see Shirley Jane Endicott, ed., *China Diary: The Life of Mary Austin Endicott* (Waterloo, Ont.: Wilfrid Laurier University Press, 2003).

Three · LIBERAL ORDER AND THE SHAPING OF RESISTANCE

1. Gad Horowitz's enormously influential exploration of "Red Toryism" as a tradition enabling the (peculiar) development of a Canadian socialism in an otherwise Lockean North America can be found in *Canadian Labour in Politics* (Toronto: University of Toronto Press, 1968), ch.1. For an important critique, see Rod Preece, "The Myth of the Red Tory," *Canadian Journal of Political and Social Theory*, 1, 2 (Spring/Summer 1977), 3–88. J.T. Morley, *Secular Socialists: The CCF/NDP in Ontario: A Biography* (Kingston and Montreal: McGill-Queen's University Press, 1984), also advances a stimulating critique of Horowitz en route to advancing a cultural theorization of "secular socialism" (as opposed to "sectarian" socialism) in Ontario.
2. Apart from the meteoric rise and fall of the Patrons of Industry in Ontario in the 1890s, the one blip in the unbroken domination of the two parties came with the Unionist government in 1917–20. This was a federal exception that really did confirm the rule because it revealed both how many ideas the two supposedly opposed parties actually shared and how powerfully Liberal and Conservative identities would be back up and running after the wartime crisis.
3. For richly illuminating discussions, see Alan Greer and Ian Radforth, eds., *Colonial Leviathan: State Formation in Mid-Nineteenth-Century Canada* (Toronto: University of Toronto Press, 1992); Reg Whitaker, *A Sovereign Idea: Essays on Canada as a Democratic Community* (Montreal and Kingston: McGill-Queen's University Press, 1992); Peter H. Russell, *Constitutional Odyssey: Can Canadians Be a Sovereign People?* (Toronto: Uni-

versity of Toronto Press, 1992). A fascinating and sophisticated account of the mid-nineteenth-century political world, which stresses the achievement rather than the limitations of the emergence of a public sphere in which political questions could be posed and debated, and takes Canadian political history to an entirely new level of sophistication, is Jeff McNairn, *The Capacity to Judge: Public Opinion and Deliberative Democracy in Upper Canada 1791–1854* (Toronto: University of Toronto Press, 2000).

4. As of February 2005, five Muslim men had been held a collective total of 179 months in Canadian prisons, much of it in solitary confinement, without charge, without bail, strictly on the basis of secret "evidence." According to Amnesty International, their treatment violates articles 9 and 14 of the International Covenant on Civil and Political Rights. See <www.homesnotbombs.ca/secrettrialprimer.htm> (1 Feb. 2005).
5. For the shameful record of the liberal order with respect to deportation as a deadly means of teaching immigrant leftists a lesson, see Barbara Roberts, *Whence They Came: Deportation from Canada, 1900–1935* (Ottawa: University of Ottawa Press, 1988). Larry Hannant, *The Infernal Machine: Investigating the Loyalty of Canada's Citizens* (Toronto: University of Toronto Press, 1995), is also an important indictment of liberal rule. Mark Kristmanson, *Plateaus of Freedom: Nationality, Culture, and State Security in Canada, 1920–1960* (Toronto: Oxford University Press Canada, 2003), provides a brilliantly sophisticated and sobering study of the security state and the real-life limitations on freedom in a liberal order. See also Gary Kinsman, Dieter Buse, and Mercedes Steedman, eds., *Whose National Security? Canadian State Surveillance and the Creation of Enemies* (Toronto: Between the Lines, 2000); and Michiel Horn, *Academic Freedom in Canada: A History* (Toronto: University of Toronto Press, 1999). Greg Kealey has written many fine articles detailing the emergence of the security state; of particular importance are "State Repression of Labour and the Left in Canada, 1914–20: The Impact of the First World War," *Canadian Historical Review* 73,3 (September 1992), 281–314; "The RCMP, the Special Branch, and the Early Days of the Communist Party of Canada: A Documentary Article," *Labour/Le Travail*, 30 (Fall 1992), 169–204; and "The Surveillance State: The Origins of Domestic Intelligence and Counter-Subversion in Canada, 1914–21," *Intelligence and National Security*, 7,3 (1992), 179–210.
6. The point about the force of qualification that "liberal" exerts over "democrat" comes from Anthony Arblaster, *The Rise and Decline of Western Liberalism* (Oxford: Blackwell, 1984).
7. For a stimulating discussion of these points, see Fernande Roy, *Progrès, Harmonie, Liberté: Le libéralisme des milieux d'affaires francophones de Montréal au tournant du siècle* (Montreal: Boréal, 1988), 45–58.

8. Nancy Adamson, Linda Briskin, and Margaret McPhail, *Feminist Organizing for Change: The Contemporary Women's Movement in Canada* (Toronto: Oxford University Press, 1988), 12.
9. Jonathan Joseph, *Hegemony: A Realist Analysis* (London and New York: Routledge, 2002), 219. I should note that this point puts me in a rather different camp of Gramscians than many of the cultural theorists who also draw their inspiration from Gramsci. I find in many cultural-studies appropriations of Gramsci a tendency to evade the sharper, political-economic edge of his analysis.
10. For a more developed presentation of this argument, see Guy Debord, *Society of the Spectacle* (New York: Zone Books, 1995).
11. For a masterful critique of the naive belief that markets are ultimately determined by a higher rationality, see John Kay, *The Truth about Markets: Their Genius, Their Limits, Their Follies* (Harmondsworth, England: Penguin, 2003). For an ultra-empirical study that is remarkably conservative in its "family politics" and otiose in ignoring how post-Fordism affects the domestic sphere, yet nonetheless highly suggestive in its conclusion—"redistribution of income is hedonically beneficial only when it reduces poverty—which also reduces mental illnesses of all kinds" (p.336)—see Robert E. Lane, *The Loss of Happiness in Market Democracies* (New Haven, Conn., and London: Yale University Press, 2000). Even more critical and convincing is Tim Kasser, *The High Price of Materialism* (Cambridge, Mass.: Bradford, 2002), which is especially strong in drawing connections between personal materialism and the environmental catastrophe.
12. Zygmunt Bauman, *In Search of Politics* (Cambridge: Polity Press, 2000), 127–28.
13. For a balanced critique of capitalist banality, see Stefan Sullivan, *Marx for a Post-Communist Era* (London and New York: Routledge, 2002), which brilliantly combines Marxian political economy with the cultural critique of the Frankfurt Marxists. It is especially to be recommended because the author has deeply internalized the Marxist concept of the "realm of freedom" and brought it to bear upon the daily world around him.
14. Of the many great books that provide a vivid sense of "living a revolution," John Reed's classic *Ten Days That Shook the World* (Harmondsworth, England: Penguin, 1981), originally published at the time of the Russian Revolution, is among the most famous. Perhaps the most vivid recent reconstruction of a revolutionary experience can be found in Peter Watkins's remarkable five-and-a-half-hour film *La Commune (Paris, 1871)* (National Film Board, 2002). For Gramsci's analysis of war of position/war of manoeuvre, see Forgacs, ed., *Antonio Gramsci Reader*, 222–45.

Four · THE STRATEGY OF RECONNAISSANCE

1. The book was Arthur Lipow, *Authoritarian Socialism in America: Edward Bellamy and the Nationalist Movement* (Berkeley: University of California Press, 1982). I should add that it has much of value to say, notwithstanding its somewhat single-minded zeal to convict Bellamy of Stalinism.
2. See Myrna Kostash, *A Long Way from Home* (Toronto: James Lorimer and Co., 1980), 13. This title remains an indispensable book on the 1960s, an understudied decade in Canada.
3. For major liberal critiques of early-twentieth-century socialism, see in particular O.D. Skelton, *Socialism: A Critical Analysis* (Boston and New York: Houghton Mifflin Company, 1911), which deservedly won international renown for the cogency of its liberal anti-socialist critique. A member of a later generation, and influenced in his youth by Edward Bellamy, Stephen Leacock, in *The Unsolved Riddle of Social Justice and Other Essays: The Social Criticism of Stephen Leacock*, ed. and int. Alan Bowker (Toronto: University of Toronto Press, 1973 [1920]), makes substantial concessions to new liberal concepts of the state by way of condemning contemporary radicalism. Finally, and most importantly, William Lyon Mackenzie King, soon to be prime minister, was deeply affected, both negatively and positively, by writings both "socialist" and "sociological," influences fully if discreetly on display in his magnum opus *Industry and Humanity*: see W.L. Mackenzie King, *Industry and Humanity: A Study in the Principles underlying Industrial Reconstruction* (Toronto, Boston, and New York: Thomas Allen and Houghton Mifflin, 1918).
4. Eley, *Forging Democracy*, ix–x.
5. See Richard Crossman, ed., *The God That Failed* (New York: Bantam Matrix, 1965). Winnipeg alderman and Communist politician Joe Zuken is analyzed with sophistication in Doug Smith, *Joe Zuken: Citizen and Socialist* (Toronto: Lorimer, 1990). Fascinating materials on Tim Buck and the crafting of a communist approach to civic politics in Toronto can be found in John Manley, "'Audacity, Audacity, Still More Audacity!': Tim Buck, the Party, and the People, 1932–1939," *Labour/Le Travail* 49 (Spring 2002), 9–41, the first installment of a much-anticipated biography. Everything Manley has published on the CPC is worth reading.
6. Thomas L. Haskell, *Objectivity Is Not Neutrality: Explanatory Schemes in History* (Baltimore: John Hopkins University Press, 2000).
7. For general titles on this socio-economic transformation and its ideological impact, see Daniel T. Rodgers, *Atlantic Crossings: Social Politics in a Progressive Age* (Cambridge, Mass. and London: Belknap Press of Harvard University, 1998); I have also been particularly influenced by James T. Kloppenberg, *Uncertain Victory: Social Democracy and Progressivism in European and American Thought, 1870–1920* (New York and Oxford: Oxford

University Press, 1986); and James Livingston, *Pragmatism and the Political Economy of Cultural Revolution, 1850–1940* (Chapel Hill: University of North Carolina Press, 1992). The North Atlantic transformation of liberalism confronted with the "labour question"—seen at the turn of the century as an all-embracing issue—can be traced in Richard Schneirov, *Labor and Urban Politics: Class Conflict and the Origins of Modern Liberalism in Chicago, 1864–97* (Urbana: University of Illinois Press, 1999); Karen Orren, *Belated Feudalism: Labor, the Law, and Liberal Development in the United States* (New York: Cambridge University Press, 1991); and Lawrence Glickman, *A Living Wage: American Workers and the Making of Consumer Society* (Ithaca, N.Y.: Cornell University Press, 1997). The three Canadian books that match these in subtlety and sophistication are Paul Craven, *An Impartial Umpire: Industrial Relations and the Canadian State 1900–1911* (Toronto: University of Toronto Press, 1980); Barry Ferguson, *Remaking Liberalism: The Intellectual Legacy of Adam Shortt, O.D. Skelton, W.C. Clark, and W.A. Macintosh, 1890–1925* (Montreal and Kingston: McGill-Queen's University Press, 1993); and Marlene Shore, *The Science of Social Redemption* (Toronto: University of Toronto Press, 1987).

8. Among recent international interpretations of the "Leninist moment," I have found particularly useful Katerina Clark, *Petersburg: Crucible of a Cultural Revolution* (Cambridge, Mass.: Harvard University Press, 1995); Paul Le Blanc, *Lenin and the Revolutionary Party* (Atlantic Highlands, N.J., and London: Humanities Press, 1990); and John Ehrenberg, *The Dictatorship of the Proletariat* (London: Routledge, 1992). There is also still much to be learned from Gyorgi Lukács, *Lenin: A Study in the Unity of His Thought* (London: New Left Books, 1970). The best succinct Canada-wide overview of the impact of the Great War on the economic and social life of Canada is still Robert Craig Brown and Ramsay Cook, *Canada 1896–1921: A Nation Transformed* (Toronto: McClelland and Stewart, 1974).
9. The literature on the interwar crisis of capitalism is enormous. For notable discussions, see William Stoneman, *A History of the Economic Analysis of the Great Depression in America* (New York and London: Garland Publishing, 1979); Michael A. Bernstein, *The Great Depression: Delayed Recovery and Economic Change in America, 1929–1939* (Cambridge: Cambridge University Press, 1989); Gene Smiley, *Rethinking the Great Depression* (Chicago: Ivan R. Dee, 2003); Theo Balderston, ed., *The World Economy and National Economies in the Interwar Slump* (New York: Palgrave Macmillan, 2002); John A. Garraty, *Great Depression: An Inquiry into the Causes, Course, and Consequences of the Worldwide Depression of the 1930s, as seen by Contemporaries and in the Light of History* (San Francisco: Harcourt Brace Jovanovich, 1986); and Peter Fearon, *Origins and Nature of the Great Slump, 1929–1932* (London: Macmillan, 1979). For a stimulating discus-

sion of the implications of the history of the Great Depression for present-day problems, see Harold James, *The End of Globalization: Lessons from the Great Depression* (Cambridge, Mass.: Harvard University Press, 2001).

10. For the impact of the U.S. rise to globalism, see—out of a vast library of titles on Canadian-American relations—John Herd Thompson and Stephen J. Randall, *Canada and the United States: Ambivalent Allies* (Montreal and Kingston: McGill-Queen's University Press, 1994). An influential left-wing response to the new world realities was a reconsideration of the laws of capitalist development. A growing body of books asserted that "underdevelopment" was the flip side of "development"; soon more complex ideas of dependency and dependent development took root. For commentary on this literature, which influenced the entire Canadian fourth formation to varying degrees, see Magnus Blomstrom and Bjorn Hettne, *Development Theory in Transition: The Dependency Debate and Beyond: Third World Responses* (London: Zed Books, 1984); Robert A. Packenham, *The Dependency Movement: Scholarship and Politics in Development Studies* (Cambridge, Mass.: Harvard University Press, 1992); Frans J. Schuurman, *Beyond the Impasse: New Directions in Development Theory* (London and New Jersey: Zed Books, 1993); Jonathan Crush, ed., *Power of Development* (London and New York: Routledge, 1995).
11. For leading titles on post-Fordism internationally, see A. Amin, ed., *Postfordism: A Reader* (London: Blackwell, 1994) for a useful reader; note in particular A. Amin, "Post-Fordism: Models, Fantasies and Phantoms of Transition." Robert Brenner, "The Economics of Global Turbulence," *New Left Review*, 1, 229 (May–June 1998): 1–165; and Brenner, *The Boom and the Bubble: The US in the World Economy* (London: Verso, 2002) are excellent overviews. There is now a library of books and articles on globalization—the National Library of Canada lists over 1,800 titles on this subject, and I have consulted only a tiny fraction of them. For brisk and efficient introductions, see Wayne Ellwood, *The No-Nonsense Guide to Globalization* (Toronto: Between the Lines, 2001) and Maggie Black, *The No-Nonsense Guide to International Development* (Toronto: Between the Lines, 2002). Roland Robertson and Habib Haque Khndker, "Discourses of Globalization: Preliminary Considerations," *International Sociology* 13,1 (March 1998), 24–50, is a very useful reflection on the term itself. For two valuable readers, see Frank J. Lechner and John Boli, eds., *The Globalization Reader*, 2nd ed. (Malden, Mass.: Blackwell, 2003); and John Benyon and David Dunkerley, eds., *Globalization: The Reader* (New York: Routledge, 2000).
12. The literature on the impact of the advent of cultural modernity and its impact on the left is vast. I take my cue from the works of Zygmunt Bauman, particularly *Modernity and the Holocaust* (Ithaca, N.Y.: Cornell University Press, 1992); *Legislators and Interpreters: On Modernity, Post-Modernity and Intellectuals*

(Oxford: Polity Press, 1987); *Modernity and Ambivalence* (Oxford: Polity Press, 1991); *Liquid Modernity* (Oxford: Polity Press, 2000); *In Search of Politics* (Stanford: Stanford University Press, 1999). For discussions, see Denis Smith, ed., *Zygmunt Bauman: Prophet of Postmodernity* (Oxford: Polity Press, 1999); Peter Beilharz, *Zygmunt Bauman: Dialectic of Modernity* (London: Sage Publications, 2000). For a useful collection, see Peter Beilharz, ed., *The Bauman Reader* (Oxford: Blackwell, 2001). For an intriguing discussion of cultural modernity on the left, see Michael Denning, *The Cultural Front: The Laboring of American Culture in the Twentieth Century* (London: Verso, 1996). There is an interesting discussion on Gramsci and modernity in James Martin, *Gramsci's Political Analysis: A Critical Introduction* (London and New York: Macmillan and St. Martin's Press, 1998).

13. For the impact of the Boer War, see Carman Miller, *Painting the Map Red: Canada and the South African War, 1899–1902* (Montreal and Kingston: McGill-Queen's University Press, 1998). The Vietnamese struggle against U.S. imperialism evoked widespread sympathy in Canada, nowhere more than on the left. For studies of Canadian involvement, see Victor Levant, *Quiet Complicity: Canadian Involvement in the Vietnam War* (Toronto: Between the Lines, 1986). U.S. war resisters in Canada played an immense role in shaping left politics in the 1960s; for them, see especially John Hagan, *Northern Passage: American Vietnam War Resisters in Canada* (Cambridge, Mass. and London: Harvard University Press, 2001), which revises many preconceptions.
14. For a fuller description of some of these moments, see Ian McKay, "The Crisis of Dependent Development: Class Conflict in the Nova Scotia Coalfields, 1872–1876," *Canadian Review of Sociology* 13,1–2 (1988), 9–48. For a more general discussion, see Bryan D. Palmer, *Working-Class Experience: The Rise and Reconstitution of Canadian Labour, 1880–1980*, 2nd ed. (Toronto: McClelland and Stewart, 1992), chs. 2 and 3.
15. Eley, *Forging Democracy*, viii-ix.
16. Gramsci, *Selections from the Prison Notebooks*, 343, 367; the concept of the "moment of supersedure" is brilliantly discussed in Jeremy Lester, *Dialogue of Negation: Debates on Hegemony in Russia and the West* (London and Stirling, Virginia: Pluto Press, 2000), 73.
17. Dorothy E. Smith, *Feminism and Marxism: A Place to Begin, A Way to Go* (Vancouver: New Star Books, 1977), 14–15.
18. Marx and Engels, *Communist Manifesto*, as found in McLelland, *Karl Marx*, 256. As Marx and Engels emphasized, "The Communists do not form a separate party opposed to other working-class parties" (p.255). Here "party" has an entirely different sense than the one that it would later acquire in the socialist movement.
19. Gerald Friesen, *Citizens and Nation: An Essay on History, Communication, and Canada* (Toronto: University of Toronto Press, 2000), 160-61.

20. Quoted in Angela R. Miles, "Ideological Hegemony in Political Discourse: Women's Specificity and Equality," in *Feminism in Canada: From Pressure to Politics*, ed. Geraldine Finn and Angela Miles (Montreal: Black Rose Books, 1982), 216.
21. Daniel Becquemont and Laurent Mucchielli, *Le cas Spencer: Religion, science et politique* (Paris: Presses Universitaires de France, 1998), 218.
22. Here one would underline the significance of Harold Laski, G.D.H. Cole, and John Strachey. See Kingsley Martin, *Harold Laski, 1893–1950: A Biographical Memoir* (London: Jonathan Cape, 1953); G.D.H. Cole, *What Marx Really Meant* (London: Victor Gollancz, 1934); John Strachey, *The Coming Struggle for Power* (New York: Modern Library, 1935); Strachey, *Why You Should Be a Socialist* (London: V. Gollancz, 1938). For debates over state responses to the challenges of economic policy, see James Struthers, *No Fault of Their Own: Unemployment and the Canadian Welfare State 1914–1941* (Toronto: University of Toronto Press, 1983), which stands as one of the most significant books to study the crisis of Canadian liberal order in the 1930s and, by implication, the hegemonic uses of the division of papers in the Canadian Constitution. His *The Limits of Affluence: Welfare in Ontario 1920–1970* (Toronto: University of Toronto Press, 1995) is a close analysis of the "welfare state revolution" in the province, calling into question any overly optimistic analysis of its socially levelling effects. Surprisingly, there is no book-length monograph on Canadian left economic analyses of the crisis of capitalism. For the League for Social Reconstruction, see Michiel Horn, *The League for Social Reconstruction: Intellectual Origins of the Democratic Left in Canada 1930–1942* (Toronto: University of Toronto Press, 1980). Frank Underhill, Toronto professor and prime architect of the Regina Manifesto, has received a fine biography in R. Douglas French, *Frank H. Underhill: Intellectual Provocateur* (Toronto: University of Toronto Press, 1986).
23. Colin McKay, "Working Class Culture," *Eastern Labor News* (Moncton), 8 November 1913, reprinted in *For a Working-Class Culture in Canada: A Selection of Colin McKay's Writings on Sociology and Political Economy, 1897–1939* (St. John's, Nfld.: Canadian Committee on Labour History, 1996), 197-99.
24. Sue Golding, *Gramsci's Democratic Theory: Contributions to a Post-Liberal Democracy* (Toronto: University of Toronto Press, 1992), 9.
25. Andrzej Walicki, *Marxism and the Leap to the Kingdom of Freedom* (Stanford, Cal.: Stanford University Press, 1995), 6, 14, 17, 38. In drawing on specific aspects of this study, I by no means endorse its tendentious equation of Marxism and totalitarianism. In my opinion the author misreads the crucial passage on the "kingdom of freedom" in *Capital*, vol.3, which explicitly undercuts his "literalization" of the politico-ethical maxims guiding Marx's historical vision.

Five · MAPPING THE CANADIAN MOVEMENT

1. See George Woodcock, "Henry Jones," *Dictionary of Canadian Biography*, vol. 8, *1851 to 1860* (Toronto: University of Toronto Press, 1985); and John Morrison, "The Toon O'Maxwell: An Owen Settlement in Lambton County, Ontario," *Ontario History*, 12 (1914), 5–12.
2. J. Donald Wilson, "Matti Kurikka and A.B. Mäkelä: Socialist Thought among Finns in Canada, 1900-1932," *Canadian Ethnic Studies*, 10, 2 (1978), 9-21.
3. For the context of the early reprint from Marx, see John Battye, "The Nine Hours Pioneers: The Genesis of the Canadian Labour Movement," *Labour/Le Travailleur*, 4 (1979), 25–56. For the supposed "Communists" in Halifax, see Ian McKay, "Class Struggle and Merchant Capital: Craftsmen and Labourers on the Halifax Waterfront, 1850–1902," in *The Character of Class Struggle*, ed. Bryan D. Palmer (Toronto: McClelland and Stewart, 1986), 17–36. For the Knights of Labor, see two major books on Ontario: Gregory S. Kealey and Bryan D. Palmer, *Dreaming of What Might Be: The Knights of Labor in Ontario, 1880–1900* (Cambridge: Cambridge University Press, 1982); and Christina Burr, *Spreading the Light: Work and Labour Reform in Late Nineteenth-Century Toronto* (Toronto: University of Toronto Press, 1999). Burr's book raises important new questions about gender and race.
4. Phillips Thompson, *The Politics of Labor* (Toronto: University of Toronto Press, 1975 [originally published New York and Chicago, 1887], 184, 109, 193, 22. See also *Labor Advocate* (Toronto), 13 March 1891; and John David Bell, "The Social and Political Thought of the *Labor Advocate*," M.A. thesis, Queen's University, Kingston, Ont., 1975. For an interesting discussion of this moment, see Ramsay Cook, *The Regenerators: Social Criticism in Late Victorian English Canada* (Toronto: University of Toronto Press, 1985); Russell Hann, "Brainworkers and the Knights of Labour: E.E. Sheppard, Phillips Thompson, and the Toronto News, 1883–1887," in *Essays in Canadian Working-Class History*, ed. Greg Kealey and Peter Warrian (Toronto: McClelland and Stewart, 1976), 33-57, a sparkling essay that goes well beyond the range implied by its title.
5. Spencerism and evolutionary socialism in North Atlantic radical and socialist thought is wonderfully explored in Royden Harrison, *The Life and Times of Sidney and Beatrice Webb 1858–1905* (Basingstoke, England: Macmillan, 2000); and in Mark Pittinger, *American Socialists and Evolutionary Thought, 1870–1920* (Madison: University of Wisconsin Press, 1993). For an important discussion of "sociology," see Jeff Sklansky, "Pauperism and Poverty: Henry George, William Graham Sumner, and the Ideological Origins of Modern American Social Science," *Journal of the History of the Behavioral Sciences*, 33, 2 (Spring 1999), 111–38. Robert M. Young, "Herbert Spencer and 'Inevitable'

Progress," in *Victorian Values: Personalities and Perspectives in Nineteenth-Century Society*, ed. Gordon Marsden (London and New York: Longman, 1968), 147–57, provides an accessible introduction to Spencer.

6. For "must-read"—and sharply contrasting—books about the Socialist Party of Canada, see Peter Campbell, *Canadian Marxists and the Search for a Third Way* (Montreal and Kingston: McGill-Queen's University Press, 1999); A. Ross McCormack, *Reformers, Rebels, and Revolutionaries: The Western Canadian Radical Movement, 1899–1919* (Toronto: University of Toronto Press, 1977); Carlos A. Schwantes, *Radical Heritage: Labor, Socialism, and Reform in Washington and British Columbia, 1885–1917* (Seattle and London: University of Washington Press, 1979); and Mark Leier, *Red Flags and Red Tape: The Making of a Labour Bureaucracy* (Toronto: University of Toronto Press, 1995). Remarkably, there is no free-standing monograph devoted to the party. Many important insights can be found in Ross Johnson, "No Compromise—No Political Trading: The Marxian Socialist Tradition in British Columbia," Ph.D. thesis, University of British Columbia, Vancouver, 1975; and Gene Homel, "'Fading Beams of the Nineteenth Century': Radicalism and Early Socialism in Canada's 1890s," *Labour/Le Travail*, 5 (1980), 7–32, drawn from his broad-ranging thesis "James Simpson and the Origins of Canadian Social Democracy (Socialism in Toronto, 1890–1914)," Ph.D. thesis, University of Toronto, 1978.
7. Of the many titles on the Winnipeg General Strike, which has yet to receive the masterpiece that is its due, see especially Harry and Mildred Gutkin, *Profiles in Dissent: The Shaping of Radical Thought in the Canadian West* (Edmonton: NeWest Press, 1997), which despite its misleading title is a series of sensitive portraits of leading personalities in the strike; and Tom Mitchell and James Naylor, "The Prairies: In the Eye of the Storm," in *The Workers' Revolt in Canada, 1917–1925*, ed. Craig Heron (Toronto: University of Toronto Press, 1998). Heron's introduction and conclusion in this book are also enlightening.
8. The leading book on the IWW in Canada is Mark Leier, *Where the Fraser River Flows: The Industrial Workers of the World in British Columbia* (Vancouver: New Star Books, 1990). A more popular treatment can be found in Jack Scott, *Plunderbund and Proletariat: A History of the IWW in British Columbia* (Vancouver: New Star Books, 1975). David Bercuson, *Fools and Wise Men: The Rise and Fall of the One Big Union* (Toronto: McGraw-Hill Ryerson, 1978) analyzes the One Big Union from the right. Two very engaging socialist-feminist studies of its gender ideals can be found in Todd McCallum, "The Strange Tale of Tom Cassidy and Catherine Rose, or, Free Love, Heterosexuality, and the One Big Union," *Journal of the Canadian Historical Association*, new series, 9 (1998), 125–54; and McCallum, "Not a Sex Question? The One Big Union and the Politics of Radical Manhood," *Labour/Le Travail*, 42 (1998),

15–54. One of the most revealing sources for the One Big Union, and one that demonstrates its broad and sophisticated vision of socialism, is the *One Big Union Bulletin*, of the 1920s. The careful reader of this newspaper will come away with a very different impression than the one conveyed by Bercuson's book.

9. For anyone seeking to grasp the interwar revolutionary experience, two key books are David Frank, *J.B. McLachlan: A Biography* (Toronto: James Lorimer, 1999), which expertly situates this Communist trade union leader in his full context in the Nova Scotia coalfields; and Andrée Lévesque, *Virage à gauche interdit: Les communistes, les socialistes et leurs ennemis au Québec, 1929–1939* (Montreal: Boréal Express, 1984). For institutional studies of the Communist Party of Canada, see Ivan Avakumovic, *The Communist Party in Canada: A History* (Toronto: McClelland and Stewart, 1975); Norman Penner, *Canadian Communists: The Stalin Years and Beyond* (Toronto: Methuen, 1988); and William Rodney's still-irreplaceable *Soldiers of the International: A History of the Communist Party of Canada, 1919–1929* (Toronto: University of Toronto Press, 1968), which holds up rather well. The CPC's own version of its history can be consulted in Communist Party of Canada, *Canada's Party of Socialism: The History of the Communist Party of Canada, 1921–1976* (Toronto: Progress Books, 1982); and Tim Buck, *Thirty Years: The Story of the Communist Movement in Canada 1922–1952* (Toronto: Progress Books, 1975 [1932]). For a short illustrated history, see *Power of the People: Fifty Years of Pictorial Highlights of the Communist Party of Canada, 1921–1971* (Toronto: Progress Books, n.d. [1971]). Apart from John Manley, most Canadian historians have yet fully to register the impact of the recent release of millions of pages of documents from the Archives of the Communist International in Moscow.

10. The best source for this, and a fascinating study of the CPC in the 1920s, is Ian Angus's iconoclastic *Canadian Bolsheviks: The Early Years of the Communist Party of Canada* (Montreal: Vanguard, 1981). For an interesting evaluation of the CPC's strength as evidenced through the circulation of its leading newspaper, see Donald Kerr and Deryck Holdsworth, eds., *Historical Atlas of Canada*, vol.3, *Addressing the Twentieth Century 1891–1961* (Toronto: University of Toronto Press, 1990); Plate 46 contains a noteworthy map of the circulation of the Daily and Weekly *Clarion*, May 1936–September 1937, and provides estimates of CPC membership (some of which can now be compared against statistics in the Canadian Comintern papers at the National Archives). No one interested in this topic will want to miss the wonderful Kenny Collection in the Thomas Fisher Rare Book Library at the University of Toronto. See also Sean Purdy, *Radicals and Revolutionaries: The History of Canadian Communism from the Robert S. Kenny Collection* (Toronto: University of Toronto Library, 1998). The work of Norman Penner has usefully underlined the general influence of

the CPC; see especially *The Canadian Left: A Critical Analysis* (Scarborough, Ont.: Prentice-Hall of Canada, 1977); and *Canadian Communism.*

11. Stalinism as a moral and philosophical problem is usefully addressed in Charles W. Mills, "The Moral Epistemology of Stalinism," *Politics and Society*, 12,1 (March 1994), 31–60. For impressive recent scholarship on Stalinism, see Sheila Fitzpatrick, *Stalinism: New Directions* (London and New York: Routledge, 2000); of particular interest here is Fitzpatrick, "Ascribing Class: The Construction of Social Identity in Soviet Russia," 20–46, and Jochen Hellbeck, "Fashioning the Stalinist Soul: The Diary of Stepan Podlubnyi, 1931–9," 77–116. The split within the world communist movement has received much international attention, and some of the North American titles have references to Canada. Internationally, see especially Pierre Broué, *Trotsky* (Paris: Fayard, 1988). For Britain, see Sam Bornstein and Al Richardson, *Against the Stream: A History of the Trotskyist Movement in Britain, 1924–38* (London: Socialist Platform, 1986); and John Callaghan, *British Trotskyism: Theory and Practice* (Oxford: Blackwell, 1984). Outstanding work in North America has been carried out by Alan Wald: see in particular *The New York Intellectuals: The Rise and Decline of the Anti-Stalinist Left from the 1930s to the 1980s* (Chapel Hill and London: University of North Carolina Press, 1987).
12. Perhaps the most useful recent book reflective of the massive transformation of Communist studies worldwide is Tim Rees and Andrew Thorpe, *International Communism and the Communist International 1919–43* (Manchester and New York: Manchester University Press, 1998). See also Keven McDermott and Jeremy Agnew, *The Comintern: A History of International Communism from Lenin to Stalin* (New York: St. Martin's Press, 1997); and Mikhail Narinsky and Jürgen Rojahn, eds., *Centre and Periphery: The History of the Comintern in the Light of New Documents* (Amsterdam: International Institute of Social History, 1996). The new sources have enabled intense debates, now based on factual evidence, about the limited autonomy of the national communist parties and the intelligence (or otherwise) of the Comintern's world strategy. For an excellent and provocative reading of the CPC's notorious Third Period of ultra-leftism, which reveals the new questions and insights that those sources make possible, see John Manley, "Red or Yellow? Canadian Communists and the 'Long' Third Period, 1927–36," in *In Search of Revolution: International Communist Parties in the Third Period*, ed. Matthew Worley (London and New York: I.B. Taurus, 2004), 22–46.
13. On "Radical Planism," see Eley, *Forging Democracy*, 240–1.
14. For J.S. Woodsworth, with Tommy Douglas undoubtedly the most revered figure in the Canadian socialist tradition, and a founder of the CCF, there is an abundance of biographical material. See Allen Mills's highly significant *A Fool for Christ: The Political Thought*

of J.S. Woodsworth (Toronto: University of Toronto Press, 1991), which should be read in conjunction with Kenneth McNaught's thoughtful review of the book in *Labour/Le Travail*, 29 (Spring 1992), 252–54. Allen Mills, "Cooperation and Community in the Thought of J.S. Woodsworth," *Labour/Le Travail*, 14 (Fall 1984), 103-20, provides a useful synopsis. Kenneth McNaught, *A Prophet in Politics: A Biography of J.S. Woodsworth* (Toronto: University of Toronto Press, 1959), is a classic; the same author's *J.S. Woodsworth* (Toronto: Fitzhenry and Whiteside, 1980), is a shorter statement. Edith Fowke, ed., *Towards Socialism: Selections from the Writings of J.S. Woodsworth* (Toronto: Ontario Woodsworth Memorial Foundation, 1948), is a pamphlet that notably illustrates the extent to which the CCF-associated Ontario Woodsworth Memorial Foundation developed a "myth of Woodsworth" and presented this to the wider world. For notable assessments from or shortly after Woodsworth's epoch, see Olive Ziegler, *Woodsworth: Social Pioneer (Authorized Sketch)* (Toronto: The Ontario Publishing Co., 1934); Frank Underhill, *James Shaver Woodsworth: Untypical Canadian* (Toronto: Ontario Woodsworth Memorial Foundation, 1944); and Grace MacInnis, *J.S. Woodsworth: A Man to Remember* (Toronto: Macmillan, 1953). Woodsworth's two major books—*Strangers within Our Gates, or Coming Canadians* (Toronto: University of Toronto Press, 1972 [1909]) and *My Neighbor: A Study of City Conditions* (Toronto: University of Toronto Press, 1972 [1911])—were written before he became a consistent socialist.

15. The secondary literature on the CCF is immense. Two political scientists have added enormously to our understanding of the party. Walter Young, *The Anatomy of a Party: The National CCF 1932–1961* (Toronto: University of Toronto Press, 1969), still deservedly commands great respect as a classic analysis of the CCF as a phenomenon sharply divided between "movement" and "party." Young's *Democracy and Discontent: Progressivism, Socialism and Social Credit in the Canadian West*, 2nd ed. (Toronto: McGraw-Hill Ryerson, 1978), contains a useful and succinct account of the consolidation of the many labour and socialist parties in the CCF. For an important commentary on Young's movement/party thesis, and an impressive statement in its own right, see Alan Whitehorn, *Canadian Socialism: Essays on the CCF-NDP* (Toronto: Oxford University Press 1992), which places more weight on recent NDP history than on the CCF but must be considered the major work in the field. Leo Zakuta, *A Protest Movement Becalmed* (Toronto: University of Toronto Press, 1964), takes a sceptical view of the CCF tradition as it morphed into the NDP. Dan Azoulay, *Keeping the Dream Alive: The Survival of the Ontario CCF/NDP, 1950–1963* (Montreal and Kingston: McGill-Queen's University Press, 1997), is a wonderfully detailed institutional account. The classic account of CP/CCF rivalry in the labour movement is Irving Abella, *Nationalism, Communism, and*

Canadian Labour: The CIO, the Communist Party, and the Canadian Congress of Labour, 1935–1956 (Toronto: University of Toronto Press, 1973). An important, often overlooked study of the contradictions of Communist/CCF relations in the 1940s can be found in Nelson Wiseman, *Social Democracy in Manitoba: A History of the CCF/NDP* (Winnipeg: University of Manitoba Press, 1985).

16. For David Lewis, the must-read book is *The Good Fight: Political Memoirs 1909–1958*, int. Stephen Lewis (Markham, Ont.: Penguin Books, 1988 [1981]). This must be considered one of the best reflections on the CCF tradition by one of its key figures; it reflects not only the keen intelligence of its author, but also the research expertise of Alan Whitehorn, who worked on the project. It is based in part on new archival research and sheds important new light on the ways in which the CCF was shut out of power in Ontario, among other things. Cameron Smith, *Unfinished Journey: The Lewis Family* (Toronto: Summerhill, 1989) is an excellent introduction to the Lewis family in politics, and contains notable reflections on Lewis's Bundist "Marxism."
17. Eugene Forsey, "A New Economic Order," in *Toward the Christian Revolution*, ed. R.B.Y. Scott and Gregory Vlastos (Kingston: Ronald P. Frye & Co., 1989 [1936]), 139.
18. Frank Scott and David Lewis, *Make This Your Canada: A Review of C.C.F. History and Policy* (Toronto: Central Canada Publishing Canada, 1943), 35.
19. For a sampling of anti-CCF polemics, see M.S. Nester, *"Make This Your Canada"—and You'll Regret It* (Toronto, 1944); William S. Gibson, *You Knew What You Were Voting For* (Toronto: William Gibson, 1944); B.A. Trestrail, *Stand up and Be Counted or Sit Still and Get Soaked* (Toronto: McClelland and Stewart, 1944), which became infamous in CCF circles and was mass-distributed by corporate interests; Joe Paynter, *We Can Learn a Lot from Russia* (Vancouver, 1946); Joe Paynter, *Masters of Misjudgment: The CCF's Record in War and Peace* (Vancouver, n.d. [1947]); Walter Tucker, *The C.C.F. Record in Saskatchewan Examined*, Pamphlet No.27 (Winnipeg: Winnipeg Free Press, 1949); Chas. E. Bell, *Pie in the Sky: A Close Look at Saskatchewan Socialism* (Regina: Leader-Post, n.d. [1956]). Canadian Chamber of Commerce, *Fallacies of Socialism* (Montreal: Chamber of Commerce, 1961), has some engaging cartoons. Eric D. Butler, *The Fabian Socialist Contribution to the Communist Advance* (Flesherton, Ont.: Canadian League of Rights, 1978), is a late addition to the genre. For resistance to the CCF in Quebec, see the discussion in Young, *Anatomy of a Party*; and for primary sources see G.H. Lévesque, "Socialisme canadien: La CCF," *L'Action nationale*, 2 (1933), 91–116; and Lévesque, *La CCF* (Montreal: École sociale populaire, 1933). For a later critique of socialism, see Jean Grenier, *Le Piège Socialiste* (Montreal: L'Institut d'Action Politique, 1963).

20. More critical evaluations of the CCF include, from a left nationalist perspective, Gary Teeple, "'Liberals in a Hurry': Socialism and the CCF-NDP," and R.T. Naylor, "The Ideological Foundations of Social Democracy and Social Credit," in *Capitalism and the National Question in Canada*, ed. Gary Teeple (Toronto: University of Toronto Press, 1972). For a New Left critique, see Gad Horowitz, "Toward the Democratic Class Struggle," *Revue d'études canadiennes/Journal of Canadian Studies*, 1,3 (November 1966), 3–10. Bryan Palmer, "Listening to History Rather than Historians: Reflections on Working Class History," *Studies in Political Economy*, 20 (Summer *1986)*, *47–84*, contains an analysis of the CCF as an alliance between labour and a "petty bourgeois" farmers' movement resulting in a "reformism" antithetical to the aims of revolutionaries. For a nuanced and critical assessment of the legacy of the CCF, see Norman Penner, *Canadian Social Democracy: The Slow Road to Socialism* (Toronto: James Lorimer, 1992). For an important critique of the tradition and the First Nations, see Murray Dobbin, "The Blurry Vision of the CCF-NDP," *Briarpatch*, 12,10 (December 1983), 17-19; and David M. Quiring, *CCF Colonialism in Northern Saskatchewan: Battling Parish Priests, Bootleggers, and Fur Sharks* (Vancouver and Toronto: UBC Press, 2004).
21. For leading international studies of the New Left, see especially J. Suri, *Power and Protest: Global Revolutionaries and the Rise of Détente* (Cambridge, Mass.: Harvard University Press, 2003). For 1960s radicalism in general, see Todd Gitlin, *The Sixties: Years of Hope, Days of Rage* (New York: Bantam Books, 1993); and Gitlin, *The Whole World Is Watching: Mass Media in the Making and Unmaking of the New Left* (Berkeley: University of California Press, 1980). See also Jack Whalen and Richard Flacks, *Beyond the Barricades: The Sixties Generation Grows Up* (Philadelphia: Temple University Press, 1990), which looks at California activists; Ronald Fraser, ed., *1968—A Student Generation in Revolt: An International Oral History* (New York: Pantheon, 1988); Charles Kaiser, *1968 in America: Music, Politics, Chaos, Counterculture, and the Shaping of a Generation* (New York: Weidenfeld and Nicolson, 1988); and Lauren Kessler, *After All These Years: Sixties Ideals in a Different World* (New York: Thunder's Mouth Press, 1990), which looks at the continuities and discontinuities in the political lives of fifty sixties activists. Also of interest are Irwin Unger and Debi Unger, *The Movement: A History of the American New Left, 1959–1972* (Lanham, Md.: University Press of America, 1988 [1974]); Gregory Nevala Calvert, *Democracy from the Heart: Spiritual Values, Decentralism, and Democratic Idealism in the Movement of the 1960s* (Eugene, Ore.: Communitas Press, 1991). Allen J. Matusow, *The Unraveling of America: A History of Liberalism in the 1960s* (New York: Harper & Row, 1984), takes a very U.S.-centric view, as do Peter Collier and David Horowitz in their one-dimensionally negative portrait, *Destructive Generation:*

Second Thoughts about the Sixties (New York: Summit Books, 1989). Much more notable and multidimensional are Doug Rosinow, *The Politics of Authenticity: Liberalism, Christianity, and the New Left in America* (New York: Columbia University Press, 1998); and James Miller, *"Democracy Is in the Streets": From Port Huron to the Siege of Chicago* (New York: Touchstone Book, Simon & Schuster, 1987). I find subtle, sympathetic, and persuasive Paul Berman, *A Tale of Two Utopias: The Political Journey of the Generation of 1968* (New York and London: W.W. Norton & Company, 1996), a very fine study that goes well beyond the 1960s; and Allan M. Wald, *Writing from the Left: New Essays on Radical Culture and Politics* (New York: Verso, 1994), which acknowledges the world context within which North American radicals operated. Remarkably we still lack in Canada one historical monograph that could be placed with confidence alongside these substantial titles.

22. See Pierre Vallières, *Nègres blancs d'Amérique: autobiographie précoce d'un 'terroriste' québécois* (Montreal: Éditions Parti pris, 1968). It appeared in English in Canada as *White Niggers of America*, trans. Joan Pinkham (Toronto: McClelland and Stewart, 1971); and in the United States as *White Niggers of America: The Precocious Autobiography of a Quebec "Terrorist,"* trans. Joan Pinkham (New York: Monthly Review Press, 1971). By far the most interesting and engaging text on the Quebec left I have read is Jean-Marc Piotte, *La communauté perdue: Petite histoire des militantismes* (Montreal: VLB, 1987), which uses the techniques of oral history to movingly and sympathetically describe the life-courses of a cohort of militants in Quebec, ranging from commune-dwellers to the new-style communists of the 1970s. For the Quiet Revolution—that complex of social and economic changes that transformed so much of Quebec society in the 1960s (some would push its boundaries earlier, and some later), see Godin, *La Révolution tranquille*, vols. 1 and 2; and Gagnon and Montcalm, *Quebec*. With respect to the independence movement, perhaps the best general introduction in English is William Coleman, *The Independence Movement in Quebec 1945–1980* (Toronto: University of Toronto Press, 1984). A classic statement of the "decolonization paradigm" is S.H. Milner and H. Milner, *The Decolonization of Quebec: An Analysis of Left-Wing Nationalism* (Toronto: McClelland and Stewart, 1973). For an illuminating exposé of the wide-ranging debate among Marxists and other sociologically inclined scholars about the social base of the Quiet Revolution, see Anne Légaré, *Les classes sociales au Québec* (Montreal: Presses de l'Université du Québec, 1977).
23. The text of the Waffle Manifesto is generally available on-line; see, for instance <www.vivelecanada.ca> (30 Jan. 2005).
24. The Waffle has yet to receive its due in a major historical study. A good place to start an exploration of the Waffle phenomenon is John Bullen, "The Ontario Waffle and the Struggle for an

Independent Socialist Canada: Conflict within the NDP," *Canadian Historical Review*, 64 (June 1983), which builds on his "The Ontario Waffle and the Struggle for an Independent Socialist Canada: A Study in Radical Nationalism," M.A. thesis, University of Ottawa, 1979; and Robert Hackett, "Pie in the Sky: A History of the Ontario Waffle," *Canadian Dimension*, special edition, October–November 1980. For an excellent collection of articles about the Waffle experience, see *Studies in Political Economy* (32) 1990, in which scholars and activists address an array of issues.

25. The CSN's most famous single document, read across Canada as an inspiring example of what left trade-union politics could produce, is *Ne comptons que sur nos propres moyens* (Montreal: CSN, 1971). Few events in the twentieth-century history of the Canadian left have been as spectacular and inspiring as those of the Common Front in Quebec in the 1970s. Of outstanding interest is D. Ethier, Jean-Marc Piotte, and Jean Reynolds, *Les travailleurs contre l'état bourgeois: avril et mai 1972* (Montreal: L'Aurore, 1975). Piotte's careful analysis of the Battle of Sept-Iles is a wonderful example of the power of Marxist concepts applied at the local level and sheds new light on the logic and limits of Quebec's experience with the Common Front. Robert Chodos and Nick Auf der Maur, eds., *Quebec: A Chronicle, 1968–1972* (Toronto: James Lewis and Samuel, 1972), is a lively and important journalistic reflection on the radicalization of Quebec labour and the rise of the Common Front. Daniel Drache, ed., *Quebec: Only the Beginning: The Manifestoes of the Common Front* (Toronto: New Press, 1972), contains many of the most important documents from the CSN, FTQ, and CEQ.

26. One of the greatest themes of left history in the third quarter of the twentieth century in Quebec is the transformation of the Catholic Church from the bastion of the old regime to a much more complex, often progressive force in contemporary society. For masterful surveys of the history of the Church, see Jean Hamelin, *Histoire du Catholicisme Québécois: Le XXe siècle*, vol.1, 1898–1940 (Montreal: Boréal Express, 1984), and vol.2, *de 1940* (Montreal: Boréal Express, 1984). The PQ's ties, official or otherwise, to social democracy are studied in Pierre Jalbert, *De la social-démocratie européen au Parti Québécois*, notes de recherche no.9 (Montreal: Université de Montréal, département de science politique, 1982); Phillipe Poulin, "La tentative d'adhésion du Parti québécois à l'Internationale socialiste," *Bulletin d'histoire politique*, 6,3 (printemps–été 1998), 84–106. There is an astute analysis of this question in Leon Dion, *Quebec: The Unfinished Revolution* (Montreal and London: McGill-Queen's University Press, 1976), ch.5. Dion discerned that what had been a marked "social-democratic" tendency within the PQ was being weakened by a convergence with the Liberals, accelerated by the PQ's own technocratic bias.

27. "Brothers, Sisters, Lovers . . . Listen," unpublished document, CUCND/SUPA Collection, Mills Memorial Library, William Ready Division of Archives and Research Collections, McMaster University, Hamilton. The manifesto was reprinted in *Women Unite! An Anthology of the Canadian Women's Movement* (Toronto: Women's Educational Press, 1972).
28. For a critical, if surprisingly respectful, handling of the orthodox Marxist position most fully developed by Engels, see Shulamith Firestone, *The Dialectic of Sex: The Case for Feminist Revolution* (New York: William Morrow and Co., 1970). Gradually commentary became more and more critical: Lise Vogel, *Woman Questions: Essays for a Materialist Feminism* (London: Pluto Press, 1995), is especially good for its critique of "Engels's Origin: A Defective Formulation," in ch.5. Cynthia Eller, *The Myth of Patriarchal Prehistory: Why an Invented Past Won't Give Women a Future* (Boston: Beacon Press, 2000) is a blast against all attempts to find a feminist-friendly matriarchy in the past. Varda Burstyn, "Economy, Sexuality, Politics: Engels and the Sexual Division of Labour," *Socialist Studies/Etudes Socialistes* (1983), 19–39, was a pioneer in pushing feminist-socialist thought beyond Engels. For a plain guide to some of the key issues, see Edward Reiss, *Marx: A Clear Guide* (London and Chicago: Pluto Press, 1997), 113–22.
29. Juliet Mitchell, "Women: The Longest Revolution," *New Left Review* 40 (December 1966), which can be consulted in altered form in *Woman's Estate* (Harmondsworth, England: Penguin, 1971), especially ch.4. For an important discussion of the male bias that has read Mitchell out of the "great figures" of the British Left of the 1960s, and a critique of the patronizing tone adopted with respect to Mitchell's work by prominent British Marxist writers, see Julia Swindells and Lisa Jardine, *What's Left? Women in Culture and the Labour Movement* (London and New York: Routledge, 1990), 26 and passim.
30. For a brilliant international comparative discussion of the feminist challenge to liberalism, see Julia O'Connor, Ann Shola Orloff, and Sheila Shaver, *States, Markets, Families: Gender, Liberalism and Social Policy in Australia, Canada, Great Britain and the United States* (Cambridge: Cambridge University Press, 1999).
31. Adamson, Briskin, and McPhail, *Feminist Organizing for Change*, 70. This book remains a major historical study of the emergence of the movement in the country; its focus is primarily restricted to English Canada. Margaret Fulford, ed., *The Canadian Women's Movement, 1960–1990: A Guide to Archival Resources* (Toronto: ECW Press, 1992), is an invaluable guide to the archival resources awaiting a future generation of radical historians. Judy Rebick, *Ten Thousand Roses: The Making of a Feminist Revolution* (Toronto: Penguin Canada, 2005) provides an engaging account based on scores of oral histories. For recent work on Quebec feminism, see Micheline Dumont and Louise Toupin, dir., *La pensée féministe au Québec: Anthologie (1900–1985)* (Montreal: Les éditions du

rémue-ménage, 2003); and Sean Mills, "Québécoises Deboutte! Le Front de libération des femmes au Québec," *Mens: Revue d'histoire intellectuelle de l'Amérique française* 4,2 (printemps 2004).

32. For an important recent study, see Barbara M. Freeman, *Satellite Sex: The Media and Women's Issues in English Canada, 1966–1971* (Waterloo, Ont.: Wilfrid Laurier University Press, 2001). See also Jane Arscott, "Twenty-Five Years and Sixty-Five Minutes after the Royal Commission on the Status of Women," *International Journal of Canadian Studies/Revue internationale d'études canadiennes* 11 (Spring/printemps 1995), 33–58.
33. In much American and British literature, "socialist feminism" is seen as a very particular tendency whose obituary has long since been written. In the United States the Freedom Socialist Party on the west coast was defined—at least by its proponents—as the centre of socialist feminism. See Gloria Martin, *Socialist Feminism: The First Decade, 1966–76* (Seattle: Freedom Socialist Publications, 1986 [1978]). The Canadian setting is strikingly different.
34. No interpretation of socialist feminism can overlook the massive proletarianization of women—who constituted about 13 per cent of all wage workers in 1900 and about 40 per cent by the 1980s. For a discussion of this transition in female paid labour, see Adamson, Briskin, and McPhail, *Feminist Organizing for Change*, 37. For the history of university life in Canada, note in particular Paul Axelrod and John Reid, eds., *Youth, University and Canadian Society* (Montreal and Kingston: McGill-Queen's University Press, 1989); Axelrod, *Scholars and Dollars: Politics, Economics and the Universities of Ontario 1945–1980* (Toronto: University of Toronto Press, 1982); and Axelrod, *Making a Middle Class: Student Life in English Canada during the Thirties* (Montreal and Kingston: McGill-Queen's University Press, 1990). See also a wonderful monograph by Nicole Neatby, *Carabins ou activistes? l'idéalisme et la radicalisation de la pensée étudiante à l'Université de Montréal au temps du duplessisme* (Montreal and Kingston: McGill-Queen's University Press, 1999).
35. For an important and insightful recent discussion, see Meg Luxton, "Feminism as a Class Act: Working-Class Feminism and the Women's Movement in Canada," *Labour/Le Travail*, 48 (Fall 2001), 63–88. Luxton (p.64) argues:

> The political links between the labour movement and the women's movement . . . came about because of the existence of a union-based, working-class feminism that has been a key player in the women's movement, the labour movement, and the left since the late 1960s and early 1970s. It has become popular in recent years to assert that the women's movement of the 1960s and 1970s was largely middle class and that its politics reflected the concerns and interests of such women. I think this argument is incorrect in the Canadian context and I suggest that such beliefs are part of a larger pattern in which both working-

> class women and their organizing efforts, and left-wing or socialist feminism, get written out of, or "hidden from history."

On Gramsci's distinction between historical economism and historical materialism, see the discussion in Stephen Gill, ed., *Gramsci, Historical Materialism and International Relations* (Cambridge: Cambridge University Press, 1993), 22–28.

36. *Women Unite! An Anthology of the Canadian Women's Movement* (Toronto: Women's Educational Press, 1972).
37. Roberta Hamilton and Michèle Barrett, eds., *The Politics of Diversity: Feminism, Marxism and Nationalism* (London: Verso, 1986), 8; Lorna Weir quoted in Linda Briskin, "Socialist Feminism: From the Standpoint of Practice," in *Feminism in Action*, ed. M. Patricia Connelly and Pat Armstrong (Toronto: Canadian Scholars' Press, 1992), 285.
38. The election results can be gleaned from the Elections Canada web-site <http://enr.elections.ca/National> (15 Nov. 2004).
39. On the NDP, the best single source, which comes with an excellent bibliography, is Whitehorn, *Canadian Socialism*, especially ch.2, "Historical Writings on the CCF-NDP: The Protest Movement Becalmed Tradition," which is a particularly stimulating discussion of the venerable "movement/party" dichotomy." Norman Penner, *From Protest to Power: Social Democracy in Canada, 1900–Present* (Toronto: James Lorimer, 1992), also provides a useful summary. Desmond Morton has written three books on the party: *NDP: Social Democracy in Canada* (Toronto: Hakkert, 1977); *NDP: The Dream of Power* (Toronto: Hakkert, 1974); and *The New Democrats 1961–1986: The Politics of Change* (Toronto: Copp Clark Pitman, 1986), the last of which should be read alongside André Lamoureux's review in *Labour/Le Travail*, 22 (Autumn 1988), 291-94. Lynn McDonald, *The Party That Changed Canada* (Toronto: Macmillan, 1987), celebrates the party and develops the thesis of its continuity with the CCF. Ivan Avakumovic, *Socialism in Canada: A Study of the CCF-NDP in Federal and Provincial Politics* (Toronto: McClelland and Stewart, 1978), is also worth reading.
40. On the New Politics Initiative, see Don Swartz, "Assessing the New Politics Initiative," *Canadian Dimension*, July/August 2001. For valuable reflections on the distinctions that continue to separate "social democrats" from "liberals," see Peter Russell, ed., *The Future of Social Democracy: Views from Leaders around the World* (Toronto: University of Toronto Press, 1999). Note especially Ed Broadbent, "Social Democracy or Liberalism in the New Millennium?" 73-93. To keep up with an extremely energetic and prolific Canadian left, the Internet is indispensable. Many activities and debates crop up in *The ACTivist Magazine* published from Oakville, Ontario <www.the-activist.org> and *L'Aut Journal* of Montreal. To keep up with the extraordinarily revitalized Quebec left, see, for instance, <www.cmaq.net/>, the web-site of Quebec's alternative press, featuring publications in French, English, and

Spanish. For a very significant Canadian title charting a new course for the left, see William K. Carroll, *Organizing Dissent: Contemporary Social Movements in Theory and Practice* (Toronto: Garamond Press, 1992, 1997); see especially R.S. Ratner, "New Movements, New Theory, New Possibilities? Reflections on Counter-Hegemony Today." Exemplary English-language bodies of written work are John McMurtry: *Unequal Freedoms: The Global Market as an Ethical System* (Toronto: Garamond Press, 1998); McMurtry, *The Cancer Stage of Capitalism* (London: Pluto Press, 1999); Gary Teeple, *Globalization and the Decline of Social Reform: Into the Twenty-First Century* (Aurora, Ont.: Garamond Press, 2000); Henry Veltmeyer and James Petras, *Globalization Unmasked: Imperialism in the 21st Century* (London and Halifax: Zed Press and Fernwood Publishing, 2001); Leo Panitch and Sam Gindin, eds., *Global Capitalism and American Empire* (Black Point, N.S.: Fernwood Publishing, 2003); Maude Barlow and Tony Clarke, *Global Showdown: How the New Activists Are Fighting Global Corporate Rule* (Toronto: Stoddart, 2001). As well, David McNally, *Another World Is Possible: Globalization and Anti-Capitalism* (Winnipeg: Arbeiter Ring Publishing, 2002), marks an important Canadian landmark in the literature on globalization. Stephen Gill and Isabella Bakker, eds., *Power, Production, and Social Reproduction: Human In/Security in the Global Political Economy* (New York: Palgrave Macmillan, 2003), is based in part on a conference on "Gender, Economy and Human Security," at York University, Toronto, October 2001. In Quebec important publications are Jacques B. Gélinas, *La globalisation du monde: laisser faire ou faire?* (Montreal: Éditions Écosociété, 2000); and James D. Thwaites, dir., *La mondialisation: origines, développements et effets* (Saint-Nicolas and Paris: Presses de l'Université Laval and L'Harmattan, 2000). Some of the most dramatic moments in the global justice movement have taken place in demonstrations in Canada. For a left commemoration of resistance in Quebec City in 2001, see the Peoples Lense Collective, *Under the Lens of the People: Our Account of the Peoples' Resistance to the FTAA, Québec City, April 2001* (Toronto: Peoples Lense Collective, 2003). For an exciting visual representation of the Quebec City protests, see Magnus Issacson and Paul Lapointe, dirs., *View from the Summit* (Montreal: National Film Board of Canada, 2002). For an inspiring collection from the protests at Quebec City, see Jen Chang et al., comp., *Resist! A Grassroots Collection of Stories, Poetry, Photos and Analysis from the FTAA Protests in Quebec City and Beyond* (Halifax: Fernwood Publishing, 2001). But perhaps as important as the demonstrations has been the day-by-day work of socialists who are successfully inventing new forms of global activism. Out of scores of projects, one might single out the Maquila Solidarity Network (MSN), a Canadian network promoting solidarity with groups in Mexico, Central America, Africa, and Asia organizing in maquiladora factories and export processing zones. For information, see <http://www.maquilasolidarity.org> (29 Oct. 2003). The MSN suggests how leftists can successfully struggle in the twenty-first century. In Canada, researchers not only highlight the sweatshop conditions under which many workers are forced to work, but also undertake concrete acts of research for activists in the producing countries: thanks to the Internet, intellectuals and activists in, say, Manila and Toronto can develop a shared expertise and gradually evolve a new tradition of struggle. In many ways, such experiments live up to the best of the old International—but with much more emphasis on grassroots democracy. For an notable reflection on the maquiladora struggles in Mexico, see Kathryn Kiponak, "Living the Gospel through Service to the Poor: The Convergence of Political and Religious Motivations in Organizing Maquiladora Workers in Juarez, Mexico," in *Race, Class, Gender: Bonds and Barriers*, ed. Jesse Vorst et al., rev. ed. (Toronto and Winnipeg: Garamond Press and the Society for Socialist Studies, 1991), 227–55. For audiovisual resources, see *Beyond McWorld: Challenging Corporate Rule*, Council of Canadians and Polaris Institute, 1998; *Peace, What Peace? Confronting Central America's New Economic War*, Inter-Church Committee on Human Rights in Latin America, 1997; and *Threads of Justice*, United Church of Canada, 1997. Rachel Kamel and Anya Hoffman, eds., *The Maquiladora Reader: Cross-Border Organizing since NAFTA* (Philadelphia: American Friends Service Committee, 1999), provides a good introduction to many of the issues.

41. Gramsci, quoted in Forgacs, ed., *Antonio Gramsci Reader*, 52.

Index

Index

Index